# Guidance and Educational Counselling

# Guidance and Educational Counselling

**S K Chibber**

**Commonwealth Publishers**

**Guidance and Educational Counselling**



**Edition : 2027**

ISBN 81-7169-566-3

*Published by* :

**Ajay Verma**
**For COMMONWEALTH PUBLISHERS**
4831/24, Prahlad Street,
Ansari Road, Darya Ganj,
New Delhi - 110002
Ph. : 23272541, 23257835
Fax : 91- 011- 23257835
e-mail : campusbooks@hotmail.com

*Typesetting by :*

**Stylish Laser Typesetter**
Delhi - 110053

*Printed at :*
**Roshan Offset Printers**
**Delhi**

# Preface

One of the important areas in education which has acquired considerable importance and received much attention in recent years is guidance and counselling. Teachers will be called upon to make practical decisions for helping students through their problems. On the one hand they face the practical necessity of organising suitable guidance and counselling services and activities to enable students to benefit in academic and vocational pursuits and on the other, they have the problem of inadequacies of competencies in this area. It is, perhaps, not an exaggeration to say that teachers do not know how to guide and counsel systematically their students. It was with this orientation that the preparation of the manual was taken up. The manual presents a blend of the knowledge and abilities required for providing guidance and counselling to students. It provides guidelines for planning, implementing and monitoring guidance activities in educational, vocational and personal-social areas.

It is our hope that teachers will find in the manual an understanding of the essentials of guidance and counselling and that they will develop in themselves the necessary skills for involvement and contributions in the fascination of guidance and counselling to students. We also hope to stimulate teachers into commitments to guidance and counselling.

*Publishers*

# Contents

# 1 Guidance and Counselling

According to Tolbert, "Guidance is the total programme or all the activities and services engaged in by an educational institution that are primarily aimed at assisting and individual to make and carry out adequate plans and to achieve satisfactory adjustment in all aspects of his daily life. Guidance is not teaching but it may be done by teachers. It is not separate from education but is an essential part of the total educational programme. Guidance is a term which is broader than counselling and which includes counselling as one of its services." To define guidance in clear-cut words is not easy. It has been defined in varied ways: Crow and Crow write, :Guidance is not direction. It is not the imposition of one's point of view upon another. It is not making decisions for an individual which he should make for himself. It is not carrying the burden of another's life. Rather, guidance is assistance made available by competent counsellors to an individual of any age to help him direct his own life, develop his own point of view, make his own decisions, carry his own burdens". Hamrin and Erickson define guidance as "that aspect of educational programme which is concerned especially with helping the pupil to become adjusted to his present situation and to plan his future in the line with his interests, abilities, and social needs."

Guidance is the systematic professional process of helping the individual through education and interpretative procedures to gain a better understanding of his own characteristics and potentialities and to relate himself more satisfactorily to social requirements and opportunities in accord with social and moral values". Traxler considers guidance as a help which enables "each individual to understand his abilities and interests, to develop them as well as possible and to relate them to life-goals, and finally to reach a state of complete and mature self-guidance as a desirable member of the social order. According to Jones, "Guidance involves personal help given by someone; it is designed to assist a person to decide where he wants to go, what he wants to do or how he can best accomplish his purpose; it assists him to solve problems that arise in his life."

An analysis of the above view-points shows that guidance has the following main characteristics:

i. *It is a process:* It helps every individual to help himself, to recognise and use his inner resources, to set goals, to make plans, to work out his own problems of development.

ii. *It is a continuous process*: It is needed right from early childhood, adolescence, adult-hood and even in old age.

iii. *Choice and problem points are the distinctive concerns of guidance* as here the individual's unique world of perceptions interacts with the external order of events in his life context.

iv. *It is assistance to the individual in the process of development rather than a direction of that development*: The aim is to develop the capacity for self-direction, self-guidance and self-improvement through an increased understanding of his problems and his resources as well as limitations to solve the problem.

v. *Guidance is a service meant for all*: It is a regular service which is required at every stage for every student, not only for awkward situations and abnormal students. It is a positive programme geared to meet the needs of all students.

vi. *It is both generalised and a specialised service:* It is a generalised service because everyone-teachers, tutors, advisers, deans, parents-play a part in the programme. It is a specialised service because specially qualified personnel as counsellors, psychiartists, psychologists join hands to help the individual to get out of his problem.

Very few terms have been more loosely or interchangeably used than the terms 'guidance' and 'counselling'. Bulter makes a logical separation of the counselling process discerned as having two phases called 'adjustive' and 'distributive'. In the *adjustive* phase, the emphasis is on the *social personal* and *emotional* problems of the individual; in the *distributive* phase the focus is upon his *educational, vocational* and *occupational* problems.

**Principles of guidance philosophy**

According to Hollis and Hollis, there are eight principles on which any guidance programme should be based. They can be modified to fit locally accepted beliefs. The principles are:

i. The dignity of the individual is supreme.

ii. Each individual is different from every other individual.

iii. The primary concern of guidance is the individual in his social setting.

iv. The attitudes and personal perceptions of the individual are the bases on which he acts.

v. The individual generally acts to enhance his perceived self.

vi. The individual has the innate ability to learn and can be helped to make choices that will lead to selfdirection consistent with social improvement.

vii. The individual needs a continuous guidance process from early childhood through adulthood.

viii. Each individual may at times need the information and personalised assistance best given by competent professional personnel.

**Functions**

Guidance and counselling have three-fold functions: *adjustmental, orientational and developmental.*

Guidance and counselling are *adjustmental* in the sense that they help the student in making the best possible adjustment to the current situations in the educational institution and occupational world, in the home and the community. Professional and individualised aid is given in making immediate and suitable adjustment at problem points. Guidance and counselling have *orientational* function also. They orientate the students in problems of career planning, educational programming and direction towards long-term personal aims and values. Awareness of the need to plan in the context of the complexity of the world of work is an essential prerequisite of going through education and preparation for after-education career. Guidance and counselling have another important function-*developmental function*. They should try not only to cure when the problems have occurred and done their damage, rather they should begin before the problems arise and maladjustments occur. If unsolved problems re allowed to accumulate, their total effect may lead the student to the point where his capacity for growth is blocked. In such cases, guidance and counselling have a very important developmental function for helping the students achieve self-development and self-realisation. Guidance and counselling also have to discharge the important function of furthering the welfare of the society and be important instruments of national development.

**Scope of guidance and counselling**

The scope of guidance and counselling is extremely comprehensive. As the life is getting complex day by day, the problems for which expert helps is required are increasing proportionately. The scope of guidance, per necessity, is extending horizontally to much of the social context, to matters of prestige in occupations, to the broad field of social trends, and economic development. Guidance is assuming more and more responsibility for the individual in every direction-it helps in the selection of educational courses, and profitable occupation, in job placement; placement in the next stage of education and training; occupational surveys; improvement of study skills, maintenance of mental health; counselling regarding personal adjustment problems; identifying the gifted, the backward and help them achieve the maximum. In short, educational, vocational, avocational, social, personal, moral and even marital problems of individual are the concerns of guidance and counselling. Their scope is indeed very vast.

A cursory glance at our seats of higher learning will show the imperative need of instituting in them a well-organized programme of guidance and counselling. Education is expanding its frontiers making it well-nigh impossible for an individual students to make a choice of courses and careers without expert guidance. Occupational scene too is changing so rapidly that yesterday's rocket circuitry electronics specialist considered as highly prized as a marks-man on the old frontier is to-day's unemployment statistic. One of the great stories in out midst is the dramatic increase in jobs.

Not only that quite a big number of students at the threshold of a college or university are in for compelling and difficult life situations-they are shy, fearful, gullible, not skilled in managing their own affairs. They lack self-acknowledge which may enable them to form realistic life-goals and plans. They lack both focus and meaningful direction. Occasionally they lose their way in the dark labyrinths of adolescence and do not know how and when to act. They have a grapple with complex social problems-living with and sharing facilities with peers, such as living in hostels and sharing extra-curricular experiences, adjustment to heterosexual relationships etc. Surveys of Indian students and alumni document the widespread feeling of dissatisfaction with college and university life. A survey was conducted by the All India Educational and Vocational Guidance Association for gauging college student's needs. Three thousand students from seventeen Indian universities responded. The survey revealed student's felt needs. Eleven problems were marked by more than 50 percent of the respondents:

1. I cannot do as well in my studies as other people expect me to do.
2. I do not know enough about the qualifications needed for different kinds of worked or careers.
3. I worry too much about what my future will be after I have finished my studies.
4. Even though I force myself, my attention will not remain on my assignments long enough to finish them.
5. I do not know how to make froemds among the opposite sex.
6. I do not have sufficient information about matters on sex.

7. I do not know enough about my aptitudes and abilities for different kinds of work or careers.
8. It is difficult for me to get the books I need for study.
9. I cannot read fast enough to complete my studies in time.
10. I do not know proper methods of study.
11. I have more difficulty in forgetting my mistakes than I believe I should have.

The eleven areas may be summarised under four headings *Study habits and skills, Career choice, Knowledge of aptitudes and abilities, Sex education*. The respondents reported that their *parents were the only source of help they received, if any, along these lines and practically no help had been forthcoming from college personnel!*

*Eighty per cent of respondents expressed the need of such assistance from their non-parental source.* The bigger the college, the bigger the campus, the more the need for personalised student services, else the student will merely feel a small cog in a huge machine! Another survey of the educational, vocational and personal problems was conducted by Umrudin and Gadri Widespread maladjustment was rated among hostel residents who showed much concern over problems connected with *study habits, vocational choice, family relationship and mental hygiene.* All these emerging issues and problems make it obligatory for our educational planners and administrators to build into our higher education an appropriate guidance and counselling programme for the development of the individual student into an adult personality, imbued with social and occupational awareness, intellectual and functional proficiency, discipline and confidence. The classroom activities, however well-conducted and well-organised, alone are not in a position to accomplish all this. It is true that provision of guidance and counselling services in the colleges and universities cannot be seen as a panacea for all our educational ills nor can a counselling officer hope to give students a trouble-free or problem-free life, but where possible, he can help them to resolve their difficulties, or if that is not possible, to live with them. To help them resolve the stresses and strains does not require a nosey-parker intrusion of privacy but the response of an understanding and empathic person and an atmosphere of understanding, faith and sincerity. And this is what is needed. Guidance and counselling programme needs to be introduced in our colleges and universities to meet the varied needs of the educational system, administration and students:

*To help in the total development of the student*: The emphasis on intellectual development through the teaching of subjects alone cannot help in the total development of the students. We have to evolve some method of helping students understand themselves and helping teachers understand the students. There has to be a basic and fundamental change in our entire system of education, change which recognises that matter how well a human being is educated in chemistry, physics, economics, history or literature, he remains a barbarian unless he knows something about himself. Self-knowledge in depth which has been the forgotten factor in our educational system must become its primary focus-and this is what can be done through a programme of guidance and counselling. Total development of the students are expected, accepted, understood and planned for and all types of experiences in an institution are so organised as to contribute to the total development of the student. That, all that a student needs in an educational institution is good teaching, is an exploded myth. Something much more and beyond this is needed to produce competent, mature and well-rounded citizens.

*To help in the proper choice of courses:* Everyone knows that so far our educational system has grown up in a higgledy piggledy fashion. The subjects which are the least wanted humanities and the liberal arts-have been those most frequently offered and taken, both in the colleges and the universities because they were the oldest and relatively inexpensive areas of knowledge, taken because they require to specified intellectual equipment. No wonder, the turnout of graduates and post-graduates in Arts in the year 1973 Annual and 1972 supplementary is 2,47,948 and 64, 465 respectively, while in all the other faculties put together it is 2,83,471 and 33,333 respectively. Hence, thousands of youngmen educated in these liberal arts are without jobs. The problem is grave in another way also. In an article on 'Unrest on Campus', Piloo Modi, M.P. wrote, "Our student population reaches the university level, having made up their mind broadly about the courses that they may have-a decision, which in almost all cases, is taken by unthinking and unsympathetic parents and relatives with an eye on a more lucrative profession. It is great tragedy when a potential poet becomes a chemical engineer.. Many a mute inglorious Milton is languishing in the dark engineering world." This entire process of herding our youths into educational disciplines unconnected with their aptitudes needs to be checked through a scientific process of guidance and counselling for the best development of individuals and growth of society.

*To help in the proper choice of careers:* We are living in a highly complex and rapidly changing world of work. There are changing requirements in industrial jobs, altered market conditions for professional manpower, the development of para-professional occupational selection more difficult than eve. The young students in colleges and universities need to be informed about various jobs and openings available to them and the requirements, responsibilities and the nature of work involved in them so that they could measure themselves up to them and develop and crystallise their occupational goals. They need to be helped in making meaningful occupational selection and preparation for an entry into them to have a fulfilling and rewarding career. The need for helping the students in the choice of a proper career is further enhanced due to the fact that majority of our students in colleges and universities are the first generation learners. In their family, they have no one with an experience of college or university education background to guide them in the choice of a career. With a right to the best education available, and a wide range of jobs open them, these students need mature help in making a judicious occupational choice. Hence the need of adequate guidance and counselling arrangement in our colleges and universities.

*To help the students in vocational development:* The process of vocational development covers almost the entire span of life on an individual. It begins quite early in one's life and continue till sometimes after retirement. In this process, the individual passes through various stages— growth, exploration, maintenance and decline. Guidance services need to be provided to the colleges and universities to help the students in the process of vocational development-particularly the stage of growth and exploration, by making it possible for them to gain knowledge about themselves-their abilities, interests and needs on, the one hand and knowledge about the world of work on the other. By providing them opportunities for self-exploration as well as exploration of the world of work while they are still in an educational institution, their transition from education to work can be facilitated.

*To develop readiness for choices and changes to face new challenges*: In a paper entitled The Need for counselling in Higher Education, presented at the Third International

Round Table of Educational Counselling and Vocational Guidance, Miss New some, Counselling Officer at the University of Keels, North Strafford Shire, England, writes, "For the students of higher education the demands of life are likely to be great, in a most different way from the exacting demands of education itself. On graduating he will be called upon to make use of the kind of person he has become as much if not more than what he has learnt in his course of study-not only to make an initial choice of what he is to do on graduating but will be called upon to change his occupation several times in a life time. Readiness for these choices and changes is essential, not only to the student himself but to the society as a whole. To the extent to which he is able to capitalise on his experience and face new challenges with a realistic expectation of success, to that extent he will benefit society. If he is unable to meet the changing demands, not only of the working world but also of his other roles of life, to that extent he will be a liability and will fail to fulfil the expectations which society has for its most able people." Guidance services are needed to develop in the students the ability to cope with their new problems and concerns in such a way that they become more competent to meet the demands which will continue to be made upon them in the future.

To minimise the mismatching between education and employment and help in the efficient use of manpower: The latest analysis done by Planning Commission reveals that the educated youth between 15 and 29 years of age constituted 11.5 per cent of the corresponding labour force but they accounted for 33.2 per cent of the total unemployment in the country. According to the Planning Commission's labour force projections, the total number of educated unemployed at the beginning of 1980 was estimated at 3.47 million. If there is no further deterioration in the unemployment rate, this number is likely to go upto 4.66 million in 1985. And this is the challenging situation we have to face.

It needs to be pointed out that the hiatus between education and employment has rarely been as wide and as disturbing as it is today. Higher academic education, as very well pointed out by Mr. L. K. Jha, Chairman of the Economic Administration Reforms Commission, is far too general and diffused to be of practical value to the vast majority of youngmen and women. Most of our young men and women have no clear objectives or career targets. They amble through university courses of learning without acquiring much knowledge of preparing themselves for an uncertain future. Every 12 months, our colleges and universities disgorge thousands of hopeful youngsters into the labour market who are virtually unemployable-despite their fancy degrees and diplomas. In fact, employers often complain that of the hundreds of applications that come in response to a single vacancy, at least 80 per cent have no relevance to the job specifications whatsoever. Few students pursue their education with a clear idea as to what they would eventually like to become. People even register at the employment exchange with scant idea about the sort of work they would like to be employed at. No wonder while jobs go abegging the youth go begging for jobs. Not only that, the employment of workers ill-suited to their jobs generally leads to a higher rate of labour placement or to the retention of persons who are inefficient. All this is a huge wastage of our scant resources. Guidance facilities can help in reducing this wastage and thus ensure efficient use of manpower.

*To motive the youth for self-employment:* Considering the magnitude of educated job-seekers flowing into the job market in India every year, it is essential that a sizable fraction of enterprising youth is initiated into careers of self-employment. Some arrangement needs to be instituted in the colleges and universities to identify the deserving cases fit to take up self-employment, educate them on how to proceed about the job of setting up a venture, help them through the cooperation of the concerned agencies in this sphere to prepare technically sound and economically viable projects; sponsor their cases to the banks for loan assistance and guide them to overcome the teething troubles effective follow-up after the commencement of the venture.

*To help freshers establish proper identity:* In our country the youngmen entering colleges and even universities are comparatively young in years. Young adolescents s they are, they are passing through a stage between childhood and adulthood, between the morality learned as a child and the ethics to be developed by the adult. They find it extremely difficult to establish a satisfactory identity. Such failure or delay leads to what can be called "role diffusion". This crisis in role identity is perhaps very acute today. The uncertainties of the future, the conflicts in languages, culture, regions, castes, etc., and the erosion of traditional values has rendered Indian youth rootless.

Fuster did a small study with Bombay college students, both men and women. The strongest needs, as reported by the students themselves where they were requested to indicate rank orders, were for achievement in life, self-reliance and a sense of security, success in college and university, to have an understanding friend and (for the males) *money*.

Guidance and counselling programme is needed to help students deal effectively with the normal developmental tasks of adolescence and face life situations boldly.

*To identify and motivate the students from weaker sections of society:* Students from weaker sections have their own problems and needs. They experience difficulty in adjustment with the peers, teachers and the environment.

To communicate, make friends, utilise the time profitably, make the best use of lectures, make an effective use of library and other facilities available all pose problems for them. Guidance facilities are urgently needed for such type of students to enable them to adjust and utilise the available facilities properly.

*To help the students in their period of turmoil and confusion*: The students undergo a great deal of turmoil and searching to give meaning to their lives. They have their conflicts and anxieties. They feel disillusioned regarding higher education. They find that colleges and universities, instead of imparting them education, just enable them to pass examinations-they feel sunk and cheated. When this education does not enable them to get immediate employment, they feel lost and bewildered. Similarly, they have their personal conflicts and anxieties. They have the problems about their parents and family, their relations to boy and girl friends. They have the problems of adjusting their personality to the world of people, of ethical ideas and of goals and situations. For tacking all these situations successfully, they need someone to sort out the strands-they need some strong, tactile presence of a hand guiding the anxious and enabling them to develop realistic expectations.

*To help in checking wastage and stagnation:* The average pass percentage at the graduate and post-graduate level is about 50 to 60. Thousands of our students, unfortunately, drop out, get pushed out, and fall out of the system. This problem is becoming more serious day by day. This poor achievement may be due to so many reasons lack of proper study skills and effective study habits, lack of the knowledge for making full use of the facilities provided and so on. Also, the majority of our students do not fulfil the promise indicated by the Secondary School leaving examinations and do not utilize their professional qualifications after graduation.

A study of the years 1950 and 1954 alumni of Delhi University where approximately 1800 alumni were interviewed revealed:

i. In general, these students did not fulfil the promise indicated by secondary school leaving examinations, since about 45 per cent received a lower university rating at graduation.

ii. Many graduates do not use their training occupationally.

A study conducted by D.G.E and T., Ministry of Labour, 1962 on the graduates of the year 1950 revealed the percentage of graduates in clerical work-commerce 67 per cent, B.Sc. Pass 63 per cent. B.A. Pass 64 per cent, Proficiency in Law Certificate 48 per cent, M.A. Arts 31 per cent, B.A. Honours 25 per cent, etc. It is obvious that sizable percentage of alumni obtaining professional qualifications have to work as clerks. The report also gives evidence of much aimless and unrealistic vocational choice. Higher education is a very costly enterprise. Much of the money wasted on these poor and low achievers could be saved by a policy of prevention. Just as preventive medicine is sounder economically and more humane than remedial medicine, so too is preventive education more sound economically than remedial education. There is thus a clear need for developing better professional services of a counselling kind to check the huge wastage of student time and money and also huge state expenditure on education. Miller, in this connection, said so well, "If one counsellor could prevent the wastage of only four student years each costing - 800 to -1200, he would be earning his keep. Similar savings of graduate salaries foregone as a result of failure or delay would benefit student as well as the taxpayer."

*To identify and help students in need of special help:* There are such students as the gifted, the backward, the handicapped who need special opportunities. Some arrangement needs to be provided in our colleges and universities to identify them and provide them with help according to their requirements.

*To ensure the proper utilization of time spent outside the classrooms:* It is common knowledge that students in the colleges and universities spend two to three times as many hours outside classrooms as in them. And the manner in which students spend their non-class hours clearly affects their success in achieving both academic competence and personal development of all types. It is, therefore, essential that institutions of higher learning provide positive direction to students by influencing how they can use those non-class hours. They programme of guidance and counselling can meet this need.

*To help in tackling problems arising out of student explosion*: Increased demand for higher education is outstripping the growth of facilities in the seats of higher learning. Resultant unfortunate qualitative changes in the nature of entire educative experiences are creating innumerable problems. The students population is highly affluent and extremely poor, educated in convents and ordinary schools and colleges, rural and urban areas, students from our own country and different foreign countries are attending colleges and universities. When students from a broad range of families and educational and social backgrounds meet in classes for instruction, in hostels for housing, in cafeterias and mess halls for eating, numerous problems crop up. Guidance and counselling facilities need to be provided for helping them tackle these diverse and complex problems.

*To check migration:* There is an unhealthy trend among the youth of migrating from rural to urban areas and from our own country to foreign countries. Unless migration is checked by proper guidance and counselling, cities will continue to swallow the rural talent and foreign countries the national talent and thus render both unproductive.

*To make up for the deficiencies of home:* A large number of students come to institutions of higher learning from homes which are not able to assist them adequately in dealing with their life problems. Because of various factors such as rapid industrialisation, political and social changes in the occupational structure of the country and the growing complexity of life there are greater pressures and strains in the family. They home is not able to provide the kind of support and help it did in earlier days. Also, there is a gap in the range of sympathetic adults who could be turned to in need, which formerly was filled by adult who could be turned to in need, which formerly was filled by adult brothers and sisters, friendly aunts and grand parents when communities and families were more intimate.

Also our homes are not equipped to be the source of information concerning the qualifications required for different kinds of courses or careers. Such information can come from agencies which make a full time job of supplying adequate and up-to-date materials. Similarly, home is not equipped for studying future labour shortages and the labour supply and demand situation. Besides, many parents are not trained for helping their grown up children to develop sound study techniques, and obtain reliable information in matters of sex etc. Seth collected a sample of students at Allahabad University. The parents were indicated as the most usual source of help. Forty per cent of student respondents said that they could not discuss their problems with their parents. There is a strong evidence that professional help could be well-used.

# 2 Need and Scope of Guidance and Counselling

The National Association of Counsellors in Education and the Association for Student Counselling are the two groups particularly appropriate for people who work in educational settings. Their membership consists perhaps at most, of a thousand people who are sufficiently interested in counselling in education to join an appropriate association. Some members of the National Association of Careeres and Guidance Teachers may consider counselling as part of their work. It seems unlikely that there are more counsellors throughout the country than the number of people in these groups, certainly not a number to be justifiably considered a multitude. The advent of professional counselling as a supplement to pastoral care has had a very mixed reception. There has been hostility and resentment from those teachers, tutors and parents who see the counsellor as one who is making a take-over bid for the personal relationships with children and students which hitherto have bee their concern. Others feel antagonistic towards the counsellors' acceptance of children as they are and towards the counsellor's effort to help young people to make their own choices and decisions and, within limits, to take responsibility for their own lives. I remember being sharply taken to task by a school governor because I said that children should not have freedom to choose anything. Perhaps a look at some of the objection to counselling which people raise may be appropriate as an introduction to the needs.

Not a great deal is known about counselling in education in this country, and one of the aims of this book is to provide an introduction to the work which may help people to decide what counselling can and cannot do in diverse educational settings. Among those people who know a little about counselling and among those who know nothing there are some who raise strong objections to the introduction of counselling as a specialist activity in schools and colleges, which is what I advocate. Some of these objections merit attention, because they arise from very real fears and firm beliefs about the meaning of education and of life, and they are helpful in the sense that they enable counsellors, indeed sometimes force them, to re-examine their own beliefs and acknowledge their defences.

**Counselling is of no value**

This view is representative of those who believe that any helping relationship is detrimental both to individuals and to society because to need help is a sign of weakness and to provide it fosters deficiencies in charter; adversity is the means to strength and people should counter it along and unaided. Leona Tyler argues that 'Counseling is still to a large extent an art, dependent more on shared experience than on reported experiments..' and counsellors need to 'distinguish between the things we do simply because they seem to work well and things we so because of some definite research evidence'. Nevertheless counsellors can and should assess the value of what they are doing.

**Counselling fosters conformity**

This objection to helping professions is being voiced increasingly by some students, who suggest that the counsellors manipulates people for example, into taking up safe, secure occupations instead of 'doing their own thing', which seems to ignore the fact that for some people 'doing their own thing' lies in a secure occupation and conformity. It is true that counsellors encourage people to take into account the cognitive and affective aspects of a decision or problems and the likely consequences, which does to some extent encourage caution. The alternative is action by impulse, which in certain circumstances, such as immediate danger, or in response to another person's distress, may be appropriate.

**Counselling perpetuates the myth of freedom**

Those who object to the self concept theories of counselling suggest that counsellors deceive themselves by talking about freedom of choice, for in reality life is deterministic and each step affects the direction of the next one. Someone described the importance of previous experience by saying that 'as we walk into the future we come face to face with the past'. In suggesting that we have a human capacity to choose between two or more genuine alternatives we should acknowledge that the choice is always limited and freedom have been compared to a game of cards, in which the limits are imposed by the cards which you are dealt and the freedom comes in the way you choose to play those cards.

**Counselling is not a discipline**

At the present time in this country, counselling is not a discipline; it draws upon knowledge from many areas but its main subject is people, and to may knowledge there is no subject which attempts to concern itself with people in the way in which counselling does. Psychology is concerned with behaviour, not so much with the people who do the behaving, and sociology seems concerned to a large extent with people in groups and the problems which society creates for them, but not with solutions. Between psychology and sociology there seems to be a gap in our knowledge and our concern which social psychology to some extent may close, but into which counselling is a study of interpersonal relationships, their effects, their development and practice in education may grow. Much depends upon the activity of counsellors and counsellors educators and the importance that they themselves attach to the study of their subject. However, in America Brammer and Shostron suggest that 'there is an identifiable body of fairly valid techniques and progress for counseling and psychotherapy'.

**Counsellors are inadequately educated.**

The objection that counsellors are inadequately prepared for their work must inevitable in these early years have some validity. It is of vital importance to assess the needs in a particular school or college which a counselling service may realistically be expected to meet and it is essential to appoint a counsellor who is trained and capable of running the type of service needed. Of course counsellors are indequately prepared to perform as psychiatrists, as educational psychologists, as nurses, as mind readers or as magicians. Trained counsellors should be adequately educated to counsel students who may wish to talk with them about personal, educational or vocational problems, but they are not trained to solve all these problems; they should be adequately educated in the administration and interpretation of certain tests, and in their liaison work with outside social services and with school staff. Counsellors are always learning and one of the things that a few years' experience as a counsellor reveals very painfully is that the counsellor who tries to be many things to many people sometimes ends up being nothing to anybody.

**Counselling is not universally available throughout a school**

The objection that in theory counselling is available to all children or students but in practice is limited (usually because of the size of the school population and the counsellor's own temperament and preferences) is a valid one. Counselling is often regarded as a source of help for those with problems or crises, but it can have a preventive as well as a remedial function, and it is only one source of help; students and children alike will turn for help to any one of a number of people within the institution, according to their temperament and inclination. The relationship and help provided by a counsellor are not for everyone and cannot compensate in the long term for other relationships which may be inadequate.

**Counsellors pamper people and make them dependent**

The charge that counsellors pamper students often arises from those who equate understanding with softness and over-indulgence, and acceptance with the sanctioning of any kind of behaviour, The understanding and acceptance offered by a counsellor are an attempt to encourage constructive ways of copying with problems rather than the negative or destructive ones which often seem to occur as a result of the blind application of moral judgements.

**Counselling is an unwarranted invasion of privacy**

'We are, I fear, getting to know one another. Reticence, secrecy, concealment of self have been transformed into social problems; once they were aspects of civility'. The right to privacy is fundamental to adults and children, and certainly pupils and students should be free to reject our concern, but in most circumstances counselling is not imposed, and therefore privacy should not be invaded without agreement. I think Rieff is right to point out the danger in the increase in over-solicitousness and I hop that counsellors may have the experience to help to balance this rather than to add to it.

**Social factors in the development of post-war education**

Since the end of World War II the majority of West European countries have revised their educational systems, attaching greater importance than ever before to the problems of guidance (of which counselling is a part) in schools. The introduction of comprehensive education is a development with which, in principle, I am in agreement, and I am aware that change is never made without inconvenience, even when it is a change is never made without inconvenience, even when it is a change for the better. Several years ago I worked in a school which was one of three to be reorganized and transferred to a new, purpose built, pleasant comprehensive school. The reorganization of the three schools tool place some eighteen months before the new building was completed and during this interim period the schools was housed in three separate buildings some distance apart, not an uncommon situation in reorganization schemes. The transfer to the new building was organizationally fairly competent, considering the size of the enterprise and the inexperience and lack of training of teachers in such undertakings, and the school is now well established and bursting at the seams. Yet when we consider the cost of that experience in terms of human distress we have difficulty in justifying it. Everything seemed to be considered except the people; provision was made for the timetable, the furniture, the books, the equipment, but there was no one in a sufficiently detached position to consider the situation and say, 'Look at the way these children are behaving. What are we doing to them?'. or 'This arrangement has placed these teachers under intolerable stress, what can we do to help them?' A counsellor is one of those who can be in a position to consider the 'people problems' of educational development. There is a significant association between the system of school authority as perceived by the class teachers, both as person and professionals. In other words, where teachers feel either that they have a hand in the internal running of the school, or that its outside directors are aware of their internal problems, they tend to be both liked by their pupils and to be seen as effective teachers. If the teachers see their superiors as remote or dictatorial, they, in their turn are seen by their pupils as unfriendly and in their turn are seen by their pupils as unfriendly and ineffective. Awareness of the existence of this kind of situation could lead to an easing of the problem, and a counsellor is an appropriate person though not the only one to develop this awareness and to help people to cope with the resulting change in relationships.

The teacher/parent relationship is sometimes another difficult part of school life which could be made smoother with the help of a counsellor. In evidence given to the Plowden Committee on Primary Education, the Association of Educational Psychologists suggested that many teachers show defeatism in their attitudes towards parents, pleading that the parents who need to become involved in their children's education are the very ones who do not attend meetings, which of course is often the case. Schools must be encouraged, says the Association, 'to go out into their areas and ensure these contacts, without which much educational effort will be wasted'. Suitable teachers ought to be given the job of developing effective liaisons with parents and welfare, industrial and commercial interests in their areas, for 'with rare exceptions, there is a gross under-functioning of the school as a focal point for community interest and activity'.

**Pressure of diffuse role expectations**

Daws suggests that the teachers' professional image is one of the most demanding of all the professions, requiring, as it does, that a teacher have a knowledge of his subject and a knowledge of his pupils and that he teach both it and them well. The increased pressure on teachers to be all things to all children, which is often self-inflicted and which, of course, is impossible, nevertheless indicates that it is becoming increasingly desirable for a teacher to have as great a knowledge of himself as he has of his subject and his pupils. This applies equally to the counsellor, but she is given the opportunity to gain self-knowledge during her training an opportunity not often presented in the course of teacher training.

**Social and geographical mobility**

This is not suggest that the socialization of children is solely the job of the schools. It is initially the job of the parents, and most of them succeed, but where they fail or are inadequate then teachers and counsellors can be the safety net between the potential delinquent and his determined drive to self-destruction against the bulwark of society. Bryan Wilson suggests that the creation of large housing estates, large schools and the promotion of social mobility have all weakened community allegiances, and that the important aspect of this development has been the breakdown of the nexus between home and school. Once the school ceases to belong to the community, parental moral training is much less reinforced by school training. As education is shorn of its moral concerns, and as teaching becomes subject to greater professional specializations, so the personal knowledge of particular children by teachers becomes less intense. As school size increases, so this context becomes increasingly impersonal. The individual child learns to look out for himself: if he acquires independence, he also learns the ropes according to the values of the peer groups and-increasingly evident-of the entertainment dominated youth culture. This impersonal effect is also increased by the greater mobility of teachers, It is not too uncommon for a child to be taught a particular subject by two or three different teachers in one year. The reputation of teachers comes to depend increasingly on their ability to further their own interests by manipulating a fluid job situation, whereas formerly their reputation depended largely on their role in the community as respected persons.

Many adults are well meaning considerate of and anxious for the welfare of children, particularly their own. However, parents are exhorted on all sides by child care experts, psychologists, women's magazines, newspapers, radio and television to treat their child in this way or that way, to feed him this food or that food in order that he may develop into a strong, healthy, stable-minded adult. So much so that the child is likely to need all these assets by the time he reaches maturity in order to cope with his neurotic parents. Some timely words of comfort for bewildered parents were give by Alexander Thomas, Associate Professor of Psychiatry at the Nes York Medical Centre, in presenting the finding of his New York longitudinal study:

1. Children have their own characteristics of individuality from early infancy onwards. Healthy child development can best be fostered by approaches that are congenial and appropriate to the child's' temperament. Most parents will have little difficulty in recognising their child's individual characteristics once they free themselves from the stereotyped view that there is only one kind of normal child and only one good way to bring up a child.

2. Any specific temperamental characteristic is in itself no guarantee either of healthy or disturbed development. Some children are easier to handle than others but the course of psychological development always depends on the specific

character of the temperament-environment interaction.

3. Parents are not responsible for their child's' temperamental characteristics. A 'difficult infant' or a 'slow warmer-up' may require extra attention from the parent but can develop in as healthy a fashion as any other child. To label such children as anxious and insecure, and to blame the parents for this, as is often done by professionals in the child care field, is to stigmatise the child incorrectly and to burden the parent destructively with unnecessary guilt. Currently popular theories that consider behavior problems in children to arise exclusively from pathological attitudes in the parents are a source of guilt and anxiety for any parents. The fact is that many, many problems can develop in children even with mature devoted parents who have not appreciated the implications of their child's' temperament as a guide for themselves. Such parents need insight into their children's' characteristics rather than into any presumed 'unconscious' pathological attitudes within themselves.

The need of some young people to have the opportunity to talk to someone like a counsellor was emphasized by James Hemming in his Book *Problems of Adolescent Girls* in which he made a study of the letters written to the 'problem page' of a magazine for girls. One example from the mail letters he quotes reveals several difficulties, none of them desperately serious to the onlooker but each sufficient to case a sensitive adolescent a great deal of worry and pain.

> My mother doesn't like us to love my father and tells us things about him like him betting his wages away, really it is my mother who makes all the bothers. My life is all

> worries as I am not nice looking either and the boys call me skinny legs. When we were doing the Merchant of Venice I was chosen for Shylock and I learn it all and at the last somebody else was put in and I cried every night in bed and I shall never forgive her.

Hemming suggests that we seem to be taking to much for granted in assuming that adolescents will find people to give them help when they need it. He points out that there is a gap in the range of sympatric adults who can be turned to in need which formerly was filled by adult brothers and sisters, friendly aunts, uncles and grandparents when communities and families were more intimate.

> 'Lacking in their own community the support they need, adolescent girls turn to the impersonal friendliness of advice columns. We can hardly be satisfied with this state of affairs. What adolescents seek to gain through writing to a paper should be available to them in a personal relationship.'

The vagaries and ambivalencies of this stage of life are well described by Anna Freud, who says:

> Adolescent are excessively egoistic, regarding themselves as the centre of the universe and the sole objects of interest, and yet at no time in later life are they capable of so much self-sacrifice and devotion. They form the most passionate love-relations, only to break them off as a bruptly as they began them. On the one hand they throw themselves enthusiastically into the life of the community and on the other, they have an overpowering longing for solitude. They oscillate between blind submission to a chosen leader, and defiant rebellion against any and every authority. They are selfish and materially minded and at the same time full of lofty idealism. They are ascetic but will suddently plunge into instinctual indulgence of the most primitive character. At times their behavior to oter people is rough and inconsiderate, yet they themselves are extremely touchy. Their moods veer between light-hearted optimism and the blackest pessimism. Sometimes they will working indefatigable enthusiasm and a other times are sluggish and apathetic.

What do young people themselves feel about their own difficulties? Here is a plea from a girl for the opportunity to talk to an adult who is willing and has the time to listen.

> '"School days are the happiest days of your life," they tell you complacently. But you're bored sick of school, you want to get out into the "big world outside", but you're scared. It would surprise a lot of adult (who seem to have forgotten their own youth) how many of the swaggering and self-confident teenagers they see around are really scared for long stretches at a time. If only we could reach out more, express our feelings and thoughts aloud. But who will listen? Only other teenagers, and they're in the same boat as us!'

**The need for realistic expectations**

Some bewildered criticism from a university student which expresses the disillusionment and demineralization that a number of them feel when it becomes obvious that their expectations of university life are a long way from reality.

> The trouble with our educational system is that you enter the upper sixth and they say you are going to go to university. They plan your life out. You don't' really know what you want to do, so they give you a choice.. a very limited choice at that.. Going to university is considered a good thing, everyone's proud of you. But I'm disillusioned. In a rut. When I went to university I thought I would get an education but all they do is to teach you a pass exams. I feel cheated!

Not all young people go on to higher education and of the majority who do not, some find jobs and others are unable to do so. A nineteen-year-old boy from Middlesborough describes his feelings about being unemployed:

> I'm on the dole, I have been out of work for four months. I want to work, I feel guilty about not working because I'd like to bring money into the home, to make life easier for my mother. When you leave school you don't think of the

> responsibility of being on the dole. I worry about a job for myself but I feel even worse about men with wive and families to keep.. People don't' realise how hard it is up here, they think I'm a lay about. But I do want work. I am desperate about it!

Indeed, he is desperate, for without work his identity as a man in the north-east is negated. As he says, you do not think about the responsibility when you leave school, and there have not been many people who regard it as important to help you to think about it.

Coming to terms with one's own sexuality is not an easy process for many young and some not so young people, particularly in the face of the unrealistic romanticizing of the advertising media and the facade of many adults.

> 'My first experience was with an old woman, she was about twenty-five. I am not really attracted to older women, I prefer beautiful young girls and young boys... I didn't get any pleasure from it at all. I was only fifteen.'

> 'When it comes to it you're scared because they've told you, the other girls have, that it's painful. And you don't really feel anythings for the body, except as a means of getting this wonderful experience that everyone talks about.'

**Ambivalence**

Ambivalent feelings and attitudes are another difficult area of acceptance for all of us, but educators in particular seem to have a great dread of ambivalence and to deny its existence. It is much easier if things are either right or wrong, good or bad, yeas or no, do or don't, and people know their own minds. The failure to recognize and accept ambivalence as normal is perhaps one of the most prejudicial factors against making choices and decisions to which we can have some commitment.

'I was frightened of failure, yet very ambitious. I resented authority because I referred it, and I hated convention, partly because I had a fear of not being accepted.' The extent to which counselling is accepted and developed depends very largely on the work that counsellors themselves do to counteract the inertia of public opinion and/or the apathy of local and government authority, Perhaps the most useful contribution to the growth of counselling will ultimately be found to be the publicity that counsellors themselves give to their own work and problems, and the energy with which they emphasize those important economic, social and above all human issues for which their work is vital.

The quality of life in many of our school and colleges is sufficiently inadequate to arouse anger in the mildest of counsellors, and as people who are in everyday touch with the plan that this inadequacy creates for children, students, and staff, we could use some of that anger in a constructive enhancement of our own profession.

The provision of counselling services in education is not seen as a panancea for all or educational ills, nor does a counsellor hope to give children and students a trouble- or problem-free life, but where possible to help them to resolve their difficulties, or if that is not possible, to live with them. I believe that we should help children and young people to cope with their everyday problems, for all lives bring crises which may be unexpected-illness, a death in a family, a missing parent- and most of us at some time suffer shattered dreams and frustrating or distressing experiences. Being aware of a child's stress situations and being sensitive to the individual thresholds of stress within human beings can be a complex and subtle process which requires not a 'nosey parker' instrusion of privacy but the response of an understanding and empathic person. Teachers and tutors have an important task here in knowing when to try to decrease a child's internal burden by reducing his workload or whn to recognize that disturbed behaviour may be his way of asking for help. Pain, hardship and failure can offer valuable learning experiences, but not in the negative way in which they are often used in education.

This does not imply that teachers or counsellors should attempt to be amateur psychiatrists or substitute parents, but that they should work together in an attempt to find educational answers to those psychological problems whicharise in the educational setting, for even when children are referred for psychiatric help they usually remain in attendance at school and have to cope with and be accommodated by the school community, except for the hour a week which they spend at the Child Guidance Clinic. The National Association for Mental Health in its proposal to involve schools in a positive mental health approach drew atention to the potential of the school as being of central importance in preventive measures because it is a community which caters for the total population of young people, it can compel their attendance over a long period of their childhood, and it more or less has a commitment to mental health goals.

The N.A.M.H. Working Party set up to review the purposes of counselling and its development in schools offered the following opinions:

1. that schools, because they have a concern for the entire child, should take some responsibility beyond that for the intellectual and scholastic development of children;

2. that current changes in society and in the educational scene, particularly the development of large socially heterogeneous comprehensive schools and the steady postponement of the school leaving age, will create for the school and the steady postponement of the school leaving age, will create

for the schools problems which will emphasize the need for teachers to be actively concerned with the childs' total personal development;

3. that, because of the needs for pastoral care and a growing awareness of them by the schools, the services of trained counsellors will be increasingly necessary as an additional resource;
4. that the schools' counselling practices will need to find more explicit emphasis on the timetable and in the activities of the school; and that more time must be devoted, both in initial training and in subsequent in-service courses, to giving teachers the skills to discharge these responsibilities;
5. that nearly all school activities, whether pedagogic, organizational or social, both these internal to the school and those related to the external community, have their influence on the personal development of the child. Furthermore we are of the opinion that ways can be found of achieving this state of affairs which will enhance the efficiency of the school in serving its traditional objectives.

Surveying the faults and conflicts in society obscures many strengths and advantages and seems to put undue stress on the negative. But these are the factors that must be highlighted. There are shortcomings that demand immediate and comprehensive remedies. Guidance and counseling obviously cannot solve everything alone, but they can play a major role. Guidance workers can reach individuals who need assistance, help modify conditions that call for improvement, change institutions that are failing in their missions, and take steps to reverse destructive trends. Problems and needs in society are nothing new, but today they seem to be proliferating at an unprecedented rate. Problems once hidden have become visible; new ones arise. All are given extensive coverage by media. No area of life is taboo. But rapid and unexpected local, national, and international changes give rise to needs and challenges qualitatively and quantitatively different from those of the past.

*The changing family*: On nothing has there been so great an impact as on the family. A recent feature article in Newsweek raises the question, "Who.. is raising today's childern?" and cogently points out that parents lack time and commitment to serve as models for their children. But these are not the only family problems. The home, once regarded as the ideal setting for bringing up children, is being disrupted by divorce and separation. The institution of the family is being disrupted by divorce and separation. The institution of the family is being attacked by critics who decry its deficiencies and suggest alternative life-styles. Working parents face hectic schedules. Another *Newsweek* article concludes that "the emotional demands in a two-career family are profound."

Geographic mobility, changing housing patterns, and the establishment or retirement communities have contributed to the erosion of the extended family. Far fewer grandparents and other relatives live in the home or nearby and now baby-sitters and day centers give children the personal attention once provided by relatives.

*Cities in upheaval*: The plight of cities of becoming commonplace. Financial pressures are accelerating the decline of the quality of life in large urban areas. Cities were once favourable environment for education and personal development, but social conflict, economic crises, loss of family ownership of property, street crime, and deteriorating neighborhoods have spoiled many of them. Vandalism in schools has increased, and in some areas teachers and pupils alike are assaulted by youth gangs. The inner city has been hit hardest, but crime has also been moving to the suburbs. In many regions, the stabilizing effects of work are missing; unemployment rates are high, particularly among minority youths. Family and community life exert a reciprocal influence on each other; as the neighborhood deteriorates, the positive contribution of the family diminishes. Even though efforts are being made to rehabilitate blighted communities, many families move out, thus accelerating the negative trend.

*Conflicts in values, attitudes, and morals:* The unprecedented spread of therapies points to a widespread sense of life as meaningless and deep conflicts of values. Psychiatry has been called the new religion. Much of the present unease and uncertainty began in the 60s, a decade in which traditional morals. Ethics, and values were profoundly challenged. The 70s is a period of searching for meaning and purpose, and is marked by a new media-wide openness about changing patterns of values. The cover of *Time* shows a sergeant in the Air Force saying "I'm a homosexual.." A few years ago, the topic could not have been discussed in the general press. This new frankness reveals issues that must be faced, and confronts young people with complexities once relatively known.

There are other equally striking examples. The daily newspapers carry frequent reports on the behavior of government officials that would have been called sensationalized, improbable fictions only a few years ago. Stories about cheating scandals on college campuses appear with almost monotonous regularity. Drinking has increased among the young studies reveal that one out of every four 13-year-olds is a "moderate" drinker. Cohabitation is a widely accepted life-style for many college students. Many high school students drop out because of unwanted pregnancies.

But traditional values have strong supporters. In the search for ways to build moral awareness, schools and professional colleges are introducing new courses in ethics. Secondary schools stressing traditional standards of discipline, dress, and manners have waiting lists. A well-known psychologist has advanced the point of view that the ethical and moral values that have evolved in human societies have a scientific basis.

*The new cynicism about politics:* Distrust of politicians and the political system is not new, but in the previous and current decades they have reached unprecedented intensity. The Vietnam War threw the issue of credibility into sharp relief. In this decade Watergate, revelations about CIA and FBI intrigues, and invasions of privacy have multiplied the questions. Lurid sex episodes have surfaced about members of Congress. National government, however, has not been alone in provoking distrust. Governors, judges, and legislators have been convicted of minor and major violations of the law.

People have growth doubtful and cynical about the sincerity of the government's concerns for the welfare of the individual. Social services, education, and programs for those in need have been cut back. Moreover, the public is convinced that the government is more keenly aware of the problems and needs than at any time in the past and that ignorance is not the reason for neglect. As a result, many feel overlooked and powerless to take action in matters that deeply affect their lives.

*Economic factors:* Much of what constitutes the "good life" is tied to the state of the economic. Inflation erodes resources for education, travel, and improved living conditions. Unemployment and underemployment caused by economic slowdowns wreak havoc on family life, particularly for women, minority group members, and people who are just catching up in the job market. The very economic conditions that aggravate social problems also necessitate reductions in services to those most several affected. An enormous burden rests on helping agencies and educational institutions, which must cope with long waiting lists and overcrowded classrooms. The most destructive effects, however, are psychological-the feelings of apprehension, uselessness, and selfishness generated by depressed economic conditions. Capable people with much to offer give up looking for work. Students spoil each other's experiments to improve their own chances of getting into highly competitive medical schools. Only a few businesses and industries agree to reduce wages so that no one will laid off.

*The changing role of work:* Many young people are uncertain and confused by the conflicting attitudes about work. They hear that the work ethic is disappearing, that most jobs are demeaning and destructive, that technology will replace large numbers of workers, and that in many specialties a flooded market will cause unprecedented unemployment. But they also hear the unemployed asking for a chance to work, that work is the path to equality for minorities, and that you have to develop salable skills to meet the demands of a technological society.

Many young people worry about the future. Realistic and accurate occupational information is lacking and rumors of shortages and overcrowding proliferate. Career plans can change in a day. In case after case, individuals who have spent years preparing for a specific occupation suddenly realize they must find employment in an unrelated field. Many programs are restricted to avoid projected worker surpluses. Freedom of choice dwindles.

Automation and technological advances have reduced the number of low-skill entry jobs, and have also lessened the worker's pride in his share in producing a finished article. Efforts to establish new procedures to give employees more status and control have met with limited success.

*New pressure and demands on school:* Problems, issues, and trends in public education figure prominently in this book. They are in fact often the same as those in guidance and counseling. The most pressing are listed below; others will be covered later. The list touches on aspects of all the problems previously mentioned; school problems reflect the problems of society.

1. Writing skills and achievement in science are declining.
2. The quality of preparation of entering colleges students is declining.
3. New workers can except considerable difficulty in finding jobs.
4. There is a growing concern about pupils' moral development.
5. The rights of pupils are being violated.
6. School vandalism is costing taxpayers over half a million dollars a year.
7. Violence in schools is increasing.
8. Lack of discipline is considered a major school problem; many parents would prefer stricter schools.
9. Schools have taken over responsibility after responsibility and raised unrealistic expectations in the minds of the public.
10. Questions are raised about the value of increased funds for schools.
11. Schools do not provide an effective learning environment. As much as 95 percent of current educational practice is of questionable value.
12. Schools need to be dejuvenilized. Break down the isolation of the school subculture, treat pupils more

like adults, and make the educational institution more integral a part of life.

*Problems of young people*: Difficulties for school-age youth and young adults are inherent in the conditions already described. But some particularly pressing ones need to be emphasized. Social and academic pressures on youth have caused increased drug use, running away from home, emotional disturbance, and suicide. Lack of involvement and commitment to meaningful work, education, and social activities leads to isolation and alienation. Difficulties in role identity arise, as typified by expressions like "I don't' know who I am"; "I've got to find myself". Family mobility generates feelings of rootlessness and lack of community identification among the young, some of whom seek a sense of belonging in allegiance to strange or destructive cults and groups. But the end of high school, the typical teenager has watched 15,000 hours of TV, and TV is acknowledged to breed a fascination with violence and a craving for instant success.

Changing sex roles pose problems for all ages, but particularly for the young experiencing conflicts about work, sexual freedom, and family responsibilities. For example, the girl or boy who has learned the traditional sex roles with respect to careers may, because of both personal values and societal pressures, find it difficult to choose a nontraditional occupation.

The increasing average age of the population will also affect the young. More concern is being expressed for problems and needs of older Americans. Major changes in social, economic, and political policy that will touch young people include, for example, increased taxes for services. The proportionally fewer young persons will wield less influence and therefore receive, for example, less attention from consumer markets.

This is only a sampling. Other changes could be listed; and it is likely that even more pressing ones are just over the horizon.

A report of the contemporary status of guidance coming after a review of societies' need might seem to suggest that the profession will supply all answers. But although the guidance profession is a powerful force, its focus must necessarily be limited to appropriate high-priority targets. Trying to do everything for everybody will result in frustrations for workers, gaps in coverage, and thin or invisible effects. The following description of guidance today will help identify priorities and outline the most important factors to weight when considering the occupation and the life-style it involves.

The prospective counselor should be aware that counseling is at a crossroads. Demands of the people served and developments within the profession have led to differences of opinion about strategies, needs, roles, priorities within the population, work certification, and degree of support. Each issue is complex; all defy a brief summarization. In chapters that follow, they will be examined in depth, but at this point it is important to note a handful that have major implications for opportunities and limitations in the field. First, there is the issue of serving as an agent of change-how actively should the counselor be involved in altering customs, lows, and established patterns of society? Some want to help the individual adjust to what exists; others want to taken an active role to alter prevalent conditions, for example, current attitudes towards minority groups. Second, there is a trend towards developing large-scale programs and strategies; one-to-small-group counseling is being replaced by training and preventive activities. Third, new standards for preparation are emerging. Finally, among other issues and dilemmas, two related matters stand out-accountability and the limitation of resources. Counselors, like other educators, are being required to demonstrate the difference they make in the lives of others, even though financial support may not match needs. There is a definite trend to require services for all sorts to prove their effectiveness; support is based on evidence. Moreover, counselors will be expected to produce more without increased support or to prove that higher levels of support will result in measurable and desirable change.

Still, it is apparent that counseling and guidance are well established him public educational institutions, community agencies, colleges, and universities. An impressive number of practitioners are currently employed in public schools. In 1970-71 there were more than 40,000 counselors in more than 90 percent of the schools. This is up from a little over 2,000 in the 1930s. The mission of providing developmental and remedial help to all pupils during the critical formative years is ambitious. The profession has enjoyed a position of prestige and status in time of critical national needs; its services are sought when human resources must be developed, social conflicts eased, and destructive behavior eliminated. Relatively new on the helping scene, it has matured to the point where hundred of graduate preparation programs are offered; standards, ethics, and local guidelined have been developed; and strong national organizations have emerged with an impressive, stimulating array of professional publications.

Guidance is longest-established and most prevalent in secondary schools. At latest count, nine out of ten school counselors were working at this level development at the elementary-school level has been more recent, but expansion has been rapid. From 1967 to 1971, the number of counselors more than doubled, reaching almost 8,000 in 1971. Growth in the middle/junior high school, post high school, community, and rehabilitation settings has also been substantial. Guidance and counseling, grades K through 12, are characterized by common major themes. Among them are concern for the total person, the importance of collaborative work, similarities in helping procedures in all settings, and emphasis on development.

The chief theme is the importance of looking at the total person, rather than fragmenting services as if each need existed independently. Help is provided for educational, career, and personal development, thus the work of the counselor extends to all aspects of school, home, and community life. Emphasis varies with grade level. Parents play a larger role during the elementary years, but increasingly counselors in all grades are extending services to include work with the pupils' whole environment and with other significant persons in their lives. Help must be more comprehensive than that provided by individual conferences; consultation, coordination, and training are being added to the direct, face-to-face assistance of counseling.

A second theme of guidance is the use of a team approach. Counselors in elementary, middle, and high schools participate with a team of teachers, social workers, psychologists, and medical personnel to provide a comprehensive help system. Even of, counselors are unique members and occupy a key position. Being school-based, they can maintaining close contact with teachers, pupils, and administrators and emphasize a truly developmental approach. The counselor is the logical person to coordinate the work of all team members.

A third theme is establishing a common core of helping approaches and rationales applicable on all educational levels. There are differences due to pupil's ages, but theoretical concepts, human relations, skills, and other helping procedures are being developed and tested to build a body of professional knowledge of use to all guidance workers. A degree of specialization is needed, but the bases of guidance at different educational levels are more alike than not.

A fourth major theme, emphasis on development, is visible in the effort to facilitate pupil development rather than concentrating on remediation, and by the trend to link services at all educational levels. It has, for example, recently been recognized that the choice of an occupation is not a single event that takes place at the end of school or college-preparatory decisions are made as early as the first years of school, and each year confronts pupils with related new decisions and tasks. The developmental view has given rise to a sequential approach to guidance. The total K-12 program is integrated rather than broken down into elementary, middle/junior, and senior high school.

In addition to these four themes, a trend toward increased work with pupils with special needs has been set off by recent state and federal legislation. The new responsibility is mostly diagnostic and could have the long-range effect of blending the roles of the school counselor and the school psychologist,

Within the fields of guidance and counseling there is an ever-increasing professionalization. Statements by guidance organizations articulate roles and responsibilities. Ethical codes are formulated and put into effect. Preparation standards are upgraded to guarantee quality services. Licensure issues have recently arisen and guidance organizations are striving to insure that counseling is represented in the formation of school policy. Taking over the destiny of the profession is an uphill battle, but leaders are making substantial progress. Much more needs to be done, but there is no doubt that guidance has established itself as a major helping profession.

# 3 Psychodynamics

College or university life is not smooth with all students. Some of the students' made of response to the college/ university life is detrimental to themselves, to society or to both. We find Deepak indecisive, Romi aggressive, Chetan romantically involved, Mohan getting into crisis situations, Ramesh finding life purposeless, Meena suffering from deep-rooted inferiority complex, Suresh finding difficulty in socialisation, Rajiv achieving deplorably low, Bobby indulging in hooliganism, Jaspal being a drug addict, and so on. We find that most of our students' desires or goals are not within their reach-at times they have conflicting desires which lead to severe conflicts in their mind. Some even show evidence of serious emotional problems in various other ways such as sexual promiscuity, suicide attempts and use of violence. Some are out to destroy the very fabric of our way of life and try to damage the very institution! It needs hardly any emphasis that students with adjustive difficulties are often a nuisance to their classmates, friends and family, teachers and administrators. They are also of no comfort to themselves. They are hard to get along with. Their behaviour does not seem reasonable. People around them cannot understand why they act as they do, often against their own best interests. Their conduct is irrational and lacking in common sense. Lecturing, punishment and even well-meaning advice proves to be ineffective methods of dealing with adjustment problems. A worrier is not cured by being told he should not worry. A 'shiftless' person is aided very little by preaching or threats. Such attempts make matters worse by convincing the maladjusted of his own weakness and worthlessness. He then has an additional social thwarting to bear. It needs hardly any emphasis that every individual is unique and every effort needs to be made for helping him to save whatever talents lie may have both for his own sake and for mankind. The central assumption of all guidance and counselling services is that all such "upsending" problems can be exploited for personal growth rather than become debilitating and inhibitive.

**Different problems of adjustment**

Students in colleges and universities face various problems of adjustment.

In terms of dynamics of learning, three major problem groupings have been suggested by Robinson (1950). They are Adjustment Problems,, Skill Problems and Maturity Problems. Moser and Moser (1963) believe general problems of personal nature as found in the college and university students besides the academic problems are, lack of social aptitudes, romantic involvements, problems of finance, undesirable habits and lack of selfsufficiency.

A number of psychological problems have been listed by P. Chaudhary in her study. They are lack of difficulty in concentration, tension and/or anxiety, emotional involvement with the opposite sex, feelings of sadness, depression and miserableness, feelings of inferiority, indulgence in masturbation, night fall and feelings of guilt and anxiety, getting easily upset, loneliness, home sickness and problems of socialisation, poor achievement-actual or apprehended, examination anxiety, complaints of nervousness, feelings of guilt, tobacco smoking, feelings of concern over meaning and purpose of life and personal uselessness.

Problems may be classified as:

1. *Adjustment problems—Poor* socialisation, home sickness, feeling, loneliness, alienation in a changed environment, etc.
2. *Emotional problems*—Frustration, upsetting, inferiority over a physical handicap or some other actual or imagined limitation and emotional instability, feelings of worthlessness of life, excessive worrying, excessive fantasy, frequent sad moods, feelings of loneliness, suicidal fantasies, idealistic thinking, excessive daydreaming, indecision, lack of self-confidence, feelings of insecurity, poor socialisation, identity crisis.
3. *Educational problems—Study difficulties,* problems of concentration, examination anxieties, actual or apprehended achievement.
4. *Sexual problems*—Relating to auto-erotic practices and associated feelings of guilt and anxiety.
5. *Physical problems*—Anxiety in physical symptoms-heaviness of head, strain in eyes on study, insomnia or excessive sleep, fatigue, headache, nausea and giddiness, fits of unconsciousness, etc.

Bordin has classified problems into the following five diagnostic categories in order to help the counselling officer to understand the significance of the individual's behaviour and to serve as a basis for choice of treatment.

1. *Dependence*—The individual is passive and has not assumed the initiative in solving his own problems.
2. *Lack of information*—The individual accepts the responsibility for making decisions, takes initiative, but needs some additional information,
3. *Self-conflict*—The individual experiences conflict

between several roles or between a self-concept and his inability to achieve it.

4. *Choice anxiety*—The individual must make a choice between two or more unpleasant alternatives.

5. *No problem*—The individual seeks to have a check up on his present personal status.

Acquaintance with and understanding of these problems is necessary to enable the educationists and administrators to help the students to some extent.

**Causes of maladjustment**

Maladjustment generally results from a number of causes. The causes may lie in one or more areas of personality of an individual e.g., they may be in the home, the neighbourhood, the educational institution, mental status, physical environment etc.

1. *The college/university students find adjustment difficult* as *they are passing through a period of growth—This* period is accompanied with heightened intensity of feeling and constant tension between controlling and expressing instincts. The strength of the instinctual forces and the relative weakness of capacity to deal with them, together with needs for independence and self-expression and special strain of higher education produce a type of reaction that is typically characteristic of young students. The emotionally healthy student withstands such strains of growing up and may even make it a stepping stone% for self-integration, but the vulnerable student gives way and exhibits physical or psychological symptoms. He becomes an easy prey to personality problems and adjustment reactions, in the form of feelings of inferiority, emotional immaturity, identity crisis, excessive concern with body health, etc.

2. *Emotional strain due to the* process *of higher education—Malleson* (1954) asserts that an element of a "severe emotional strain is implicit in the process of higher education itself." For the growing adolescent, there is already a tremendous, biological load to which he tries to adjust and to this struggle within is added the additional load of competing in the mastery of a subject or subjects. Learning is essentially a faculty of the prepubertal stage of development and on gaining physical maturity, the man in the more natural state wants to become independent and to get settled in life. His modus *operandi* becomes outgoing rather than intaking. But by prolonging this period of learning taking in, youth is per force to continue with a period of psychological childhood. "It is this discordance, inevitable in a modern society, which... is the implicit difficulty of the student." He feels bewildered and finds difficult to adjust,

3. *Somatization, obsessive ruminations and sexual conflicts* are *due to* poor *life adjustment* in *their previous history of physical* or *psychological illness*—It is believed that for such problems, the scene is set long before the man or woman arrives at the university as Davy comments. Mostly they have a personal predisposition, which is precipitated in an anxiety reaction in the course of their adjusting to the complex social milieu of the university. Their present problems are "problems of illness-prone young people who happen to be students rather than that confront individuals because they are students."

4. *The community in which the students live also contributes to the behaviour problems*—The neighbourhood is said to be an important conditioner of a student's behaviour. Many of our

youngsters develop delinquencies because such patterns of behaviour are available in their neighbourhood-patterns like lying, stealing, obscene talk and promiscuous sex interest.

5. *Defective home discipline also, is, to a great extent, responsible for the feeling of insecurity*—Cyril Burt says, "Of all environmental conditions the group showing the closest connection with crime, consists of those who may be summed up under the head of defective discipline.. Excessive punishment imposed by a parent-may at once call forth some challenging counter stroke either by swift and open retaliation as in physical assault or instant Right from home, or by obvious ways and hidden mental processes as in reactions more indirect like theft, embezzlement or a dissolute life."

6. *Some mental causes are also responsible for maladjustment*—Quite a few students cut classes, manage proxies, because they find the college/ university environments dull, monotonous and Vninteresting. Unwieldy classes, poor teaching, lack of pupil-teacher contact, encourage defeatism and embarrassment. The poor achievement of students is highly correlated with the incidence of maladjustment. The weak student finding lectures beyond his powers of assimilation, cuts classes, runs away from college/university, forms a gang, and indulges in all sorts of antisocial acts. Such a student is also likely to be quarrelsome, bully and unstable.

The talented and the gifted too does not get sufficient food for thought as our teaching is beamed to the mythical average. Highly creative students are generally in a fix they must either repress their creativity or learn to cope with the tensions which arise from being in a minority. Loneliness, conflicts and other problems of adjustment come in the wake of this breakdown.

7. *Lack of adequate and positive outlets for youthful energies*—is another important cause of maladjustment among college and university students. Majority of the students are not involved in the activities and being unoccupied most of the time, become an easy prey to various antisocial activities.

8. *Financial worries haunt some of the students*—and they find adjustment difficult. There are not very many facilities and openings for earning while learning. Financial problems weigh heavily with some of the students; concentration on studies becomes difficult; achievement becomes low leading to so many problems of adjustment.

9. *Lack of the facility of guidance and counselling is also a major cause of student problems*—Students find no one to turn to for their personal problems. They are not well equipped with effective study habits and do not get guidance to improve their achievements. They are not satisfied with educational and vocational choices and do not find someone who could help them to have a bearing.

10. *Lack of effective communication between the faculty and the students—The* large increase in the number of students has made personal contacts between the teacher and the taught more difficult and consequently it has led to a steep decline in intercommunication. Misgivings, misapprehensions and even legitimate grievances do not come to the notice of either teacher or educational administrators.

**Some problems of adjustment**

1. *Aggression.* It is a behavioural trait of forceful or hostile action against a person, group or subjects which is supposed to release the tension of the aggressor or help the aggressor obtain something that he desires by establishing fear in the individual or group being attacked. There are persistent symptoms of violent and destructive behaviour; the individual hits others, throws or breaks things, quarrels or uses abusive language, creates scenes. Aggressive individuals are in conflict with all forms of authority and are at war with teachers, classmates and society at large. They do not do well in studies and are not responsive to the natural demands of the people around them. Their attitude is that of hostility, suspicion and revengefulness and they look upon others as enemies. Such individuals, superficially, give the impression of great strength, fearlessness and arrogance, but they are often very fearful and uncertain. They are internally disturbed and insecure. Aggressiveness has another side also. It may express itself in ambition and initiative and thus the individual finds the means to release tensions developed as a result of frustrations. Such type of aggressiveness is desirable and needs to be cultivated. But when it means hostility, resentment or hatred against others, it needs to be brought under control.

So many causes may be responsible for aggression in adolescents:

i. It may be due to the inferiority feelings derived from physical or intellectual inadequacy, as a result of which the adolescent feels unaccepted and rejected by the group and this prevents him from holding his own with his contemporaries.

ii. The individual who feels awkward in his group due to a certain drawback, deficiency or stigma is also likely to be spiteful, since he does not feel adjusted to his surroundings and feels very insecure.

iii. An individual who feels dominated by elders tries to wreck vengeance by inflicting punishment upon others who are weaker and smaller than himself. His aggression and hostility against the dominating elders finds expression in dealing with the more helpless and the weak.

iv. Aggressiveness may be caused by a desire to attract attention in order to find compensation for insecurity.

v. Aggressiveness may be an escape from an intolerable situation and deep resentment against treatment as found in a majority of step children, orphans, or unwanted and adopted children. Such individuals finding themselves unwanted and unloved become hostile and prone to defiance and show of temper.

vi. Aggressiveness may result from jealousy of a brother or sister due to discriminating and preferential treatment as parents sometimes pay more attention to one child whom they also show up as an example of good behaviour or scholastic success to the other.

vii. Aggressiveness may be caused due to repeated failure either because the task is beyond his capacity or his method of work is defective or there is lack of proper guidance and other working facilities.

viii. Repressive atmosphere in the institutions can also give rise to aggressiveness in the adolescents.

The best way to deal with aggression is by reducing the individual's feelings of insecurity and inadequacy.

His motives behind aggression should be understood. He should be given the assurance by words and actions that he is understood and wanted. Teachers and parents should join hands and create confidence in the adolescent. Punishment, nagging and lecturing will not help. Some healthy outlets in the form of competitions in curricular and co-curricular activities should be provided for release of surplus energy and profitable occupation.

2. *Playing proxy*. This is a very common behaviour problem among college and university students. A minimum percentage of attendance (say 60 per cent to 80 per cent) is required to make the student eligible for preparing in a university examination. Some students absent themselves from the classes and their friends answer their roll calls. Absence of students from classes may be due to some causes as:
   i. The student is not interested in the subject but wants, to qualify for sitting in the examination for that subject to gain a degree.
   ii. The students may have developed a dislike or scare of the teacher or the subject being taught.
   iii. The student may have planned some adventurous experience--say going to a movie, an excursion, seeing a friend, etc. during the period.
   iv. When the teacher only thinks of roll numbers and does not know the names or is not familiar with the students he/she teaches, there is a tendency among the students to dodge the teacher.

The students who generally cut classes, need to be identified, their urge causing the same needs to be unearthed. The teacher should try to know the students by names and faces, and make them feet wanted and important. Teaching needs to be made student-centred in which every student has got something to contribute.

This will help us to remove or at least decrease the incidence of the evil.

3. *Low achievement—Low achievement* among the college and university students is one of the major problems of adjustment. The failure rate in, Indian universities, is to the tune of 43 per cent to 50 per cent both at the college and the postgraduate level. It needs hardly be pointed out that the phenomenon of failure is not only frustrating to the student but also is wasteful to the community in terms of the misspent time of teachers and loss of opportunity to some other deserving students.

Attempts have been made to find out the causes of low achievement among the college and university students. In recent years, great importance has been attached to the role of non-intellectual factors in determining the academic achievement of students. Some recent studies made in Britain, notably that of Lucas, Kelvin and their associates, Davidson *et al.*, Ryle and Lunghi and Kapoor, have brought out the importance of intelligence, aptitude and other dynamic factors as determinants of student performance. An American review of literature by Sexton contains detailed information on the *intellectual and non-intellectual* factors affecting scholarship. The student's high school performance, age at entry, study habits, participation in co-curricular activities, physical health, personality and emotional factors have been found to effect student's academic performance.

In our country two significant studies have been made by N.N. Wig and R.N. Nagpal. The study--Why students Fail--a psychosocial study of low achievers done by N.N. Wig and R.N. Nagpal tried to investigate into the significance of emotional and psychosocial factors in determining the students' academic performance at the university level. Another study done by the same authors also tried to investigate into the non-intellectual factors associated with academic achievement in university students.

Efforts have been made by various workers to determine what factors or combination of factors are associated with success and failure of the university student. The consensus of opinion among these workers seem to be that it is virtually impossible to postulate a single cause for student success or failure. In general, it may be said that the student with poor intellectual equipment, lack of persistence, bad home conditions, and ill-equipped residential accommodation is at a high risk to fail. Besides, there are intellectual, emotional and environmental factors, habits, attitudes and motives which contribute to the overall poor performance. In a study done by Nagpal and Wig, a group of students who failed in the university examination and rejoined were interviewed and also given personality tests. On the basis of the findings, a cohort of a year's intake in the Punjab University, Chandigarh were administered structured questionnaire covering a wide variety of non-intellectual and semi-intellectual factors. The study has revealed significant information regarding the causes of poor achievement.

*Personal factors*—The low achievers are more represented in the older age group. It might be due to a number of factors the students had failure or break m study in school or college; or it is just possible that these students started their studies late due to socioeconomic reasons or family traditions. The incidence of low achievement increases with advance in age.

*Semi-iniellectual factors*--Low achievement in the college or university can also be due to the fact that the achievement in the school or college was not satisfactory.

For instance, they may have a previous history of failure or break in study during school or college. A student with previous background of failure is more prone or is a high risk. Possibly, every failure in examination takes away a part of one's ego strength; effecting one's self-confidence and the ability to cope constructively with the academic challenges of higher education.

*Socioeconomic factors.* The education of parents also effects the achievement of the children. The parents of a high percentage of low-achievers belong to business or agricultural occupations, because higher education and academic achievement are not deeply ingrained in their value system.

*School and college adjustment*—Poor achievement can also be due to unhappy relations with teachers at school or college. The strained relations with teachers or even peers can be the causes of low achievements.

*Complacency among low-achievers*—Low achievers are comparatively less critical and are more complacent. Their expectations are not high; they feel satisfied with lower teaching standards, ordinary library/laboratory facilities and low participation in extracurricular activities. No wonder, their overall achievement is low.

*Personal difficulties*—Financial difficulties, difficulties of accommodation etc. can be a cause of low achievement.

*Inconsistent study habits and poor preparation* also are significant causes of poor achievement. Most of the times, students are not well-oriented regarding the methods of preparing for examinations and taking them. No wonder, their achievement is low. The poor achiever is comparatively older, comes from less educated parents, is inadequately motivated, is inconsistent in studies, and has a poor academic record as well as poor previous adjustment, is complacent and not well-integrated emotionally.'

**What needs to be done?**

Steps should be taken to encourage teacher-pupil intimacy. Selective system of admission needs to be followed so that the potential underachievers do not get admitted. Standardised entrance tests need to be devised as is being done in case of admissions to the professional colleges. Dichotomy between the media of instruction should end to improve the achievement of student at the college and university level.

As examinations and education go together, drastic changes need to be made for assessing what has been taught to the students. Techniques like tutorial work, periodical internal tests should be introduced and teacher should pay personal attention to students. Semester system should be introduced as teachers under the system take greater interest in the students and much cordiality exists between the two. Courses of study should be subjected to periodic review to remove the deadwood and meet the requirements of changing times. Poor performers should be dropped as their retention on the campus is not only damaging to themselves but to the entire system.

4. *Drug Addiction*--University and college students have been found prone to the use of different habit-forming and mood-altering drugs. Drugs are taken without medical prescription. According to the study done by Verma, Ghosh and Wig, there may be anywhere between 150 to 200 students who can be diagnosed to be suffering 'from drug dependence in a university campus of 10,000. The number is too large to be dismissed lightly.

In the study done by the same authors, it was found that out of 76 students in the Junior Group, 9 (11.84 per cent) admitted having taken one or more of the drugs at sometime. So did 68 (20.48 per cent) out of 332 in the 'Senior Group'. Thus 77 (18.87 per cent) out of 408 students admitted of drug abuse at sometime in the past.

Studies have shown that students take Barbiturates, Amphetamines, Cannabis preparations, Mandrex and L.S.D. The use of alcohol too is fairly common amongst college and university students. Curiosity is the most commonly given reason for having initiated the use of Mandrex and Cannabis and to help study or to get through an examination in case of phetamines. The incidence of drug addiction is more in the case of medical college students than in the case of other students. In a study conducted in Lucknow, Thacore et al. 0 97 1) showed that 12 out of 57 medical students (21 per cent) who sought psychiatrist help over a period of four years had a history of drug abuse at sometime. Out of these 12, 8 had used Amphetamine, 3 alcohol, one alcohol plus Cannabis. The 5 per cent students who sought psychiatric help represented I per cent of the total medical student population.

Medical students are more prone to drug addiction. Easy opportunity is perhaps part of the answer but psychological factors seem equally important. Doctors by temperament and training dislike taking up the patients' role and are reluctant to seek help like other people. Bottled up tension turns to drug addiction.'

The study done by Verma, Ghosh and Wig reveals that age, marital status, religion, background (i.e. urban vs. rural), educational level of fathers, family history of drug abuse and scholastic performance since Matriculation does not contribute in Any way to drug abuse. The urban student being more knowledgeable and sophisticated generally as regards drugs indulges in their use. It is also possible that due to greater familiarity and contact with the so-called 'western' culture that urban student takes drugs. As far as the student coming from the rural background is concerned, it can be argued that perhaps his naivete makes him more susceptible to the influence of urban subculture. It can be said that he is more gullible and easily led, and hence more easily initiated into the drug culture. It can be' argued that the factors operating towards drug abuse upon the two groups of students may more or less equalise. It has also come to light that more of male students are drug addicts. This can perhaps be attributed to greater amount of inhibitions displayed by the female sex generally in our country. Students resort to drugs due to various reasons:

i. as a means of escape from day-to-day problems;

ii. as a means of thrill-inducing experiences;

iii. as a means of establishing one's masculinity, a sense of power and bravado; and

iv. as a means of ensuring modernity in outlook and behaviour.

The use of drugs often spreads because of peer pressure. Individuals may be led to use drugs because among their friends or college mates it has become acceptable or desirable to do so. Dependence on drug constitutes a serious threat to both physical and mental health. The experience of exhilaration the so-called 'kicks' they are supposed to give, are false and short-lived. These drugs, in fact, are slow poisons that enter the nerves and the body. Acting as nerve depressants, they slow down the action of the brain and nervous system. Reasoning power, concentration and efficiency in general are greatly impaired by their frequent or regular consumption. Though their intake seems to provide relief from psychological and physical strains, it is, in fact, perception of these which is greatly dulled and hence, the relief that they seem to provide is only temporary. Intake of drugs diminishes appetite considerably and brings about some definite change in appearance. Drooping eyelids, flushed face, pale emaciated looks replace bright and blooming appearance. Drug addiction damages personality, disrupts relationships, and denies human potential.

A firm stand against drugs on a peer group basis can help reverse the tendency of drug taking and carry the message that "everybody" is not doing it. College/ University community is made up of students; by promoting responsible attitudes among individuals, an entire student community can become enlightened. Older students can talk to younger students in factual, objective language about the hazards of drug use. Such talks can *focus* on dispelling the myths and misconceptions which create the impression that certain so-called "soft" drugs are not harmful and can be used without consequences.

Counselling of drug addicts is necessary intimate relations of teachers with students can also help. In cases of serious drug addiction, psychiatric help is needed.

5. *Unrest or Indiscipline:* Unrest or indiscipline among students is becoming a common phenomenon in the institutions *of* higher learning. Students walk out of the classes and examination halls, hold demonstrations, take out angry processions with the shouting of *murdabad, hai hai* for a Vice-Chancellor, a registrar, a principal, a lecturer-declare hunger strikes and lockouts; lock the classrooms and administrative blocks; smash crockery in hostels because they cannot get food there at reduced rates; set cinema halls ablaze because they cannot obtain tickets at concessional rates; stage *dharnas* and *gherao* the V.C.s; enter into clashes with police; assault the faculty members and jeer at them.

> Frequent, wayward, unreasonable, permissive, neurotic and unruly behaviour of the youth is becoming the rule and not the exception, so to say. These are all alarming symptoms of something wrong with our college and university student

Education in India is not maintaining itself but is expanding. The ratio of students to opportunities is rapidly changing. The total college and university enrolment has increased from 1950-54 from 2,00,000 to 34,00,000 in 1978-79. Overcrowding, insufficiently qualified staff and that too in inadequate numbers, poor buildings, ill-equipped libraries and laboratories and unsatisfactory playing fields have led to a deterioration in academic standards and have diminished the students' interest in studies leading to antisocial and anti-educational activities. Lack of the process of elimination is one of the important causes of student unrest. No Indian students are dropped from college or university for poor performance alone. Somehow this is thought of as damaging to prestige. But we forget that many more students are damaged and far more seriously and permanently by retaining them on campus almost for ever. These underachievers, having nothing serious to do, become the sources of indiscipline.

Social and psychological distance between the students and the teacher (as contrasted in ancient times when the *guru* personally guided the student) is another important factor for unrest among students. Due to this distance, the teachers seldom come to know the needs of the students till they erupt in the form of strikes and *dharnas*. Moreover, during the rapid expansion of education, many unqualified teachers entered the profession and their presence has a demoralising effect on student body. Chanchal Sarkar has given an apt description of the campus of our universities and colleges when he says, here "the demoralised teach the disgruntled." Intrigues and corruption have penetrated into the institutions of higher learning. When members of the staff and higher education authorities start washing the dirty linen in the public, the dignity of the seats of learning receives a severe blow. Students lose respect for the *guru* who fight pitched battles. They too start siding with this or that teacher and the way is prepared for indiscipline. Careerism among the faculty and the achievement of the goal via politicians rob the institutions of the academic excellence. Neither the scholarly attitudes develop among teachers nor do the students develop interest in studies, hence they start taking interest in non-academic pursuits, leading to indiscipline. The students in our colleges and universities have leisure, plenty of it. The educational system does not force them to work hard during the academic year. Students have little to do during innumerable holiday. Part time jobs are not available in large numbers. An idle brain is the devil's workshop-no wonder indisciplinary acts dominate the campuses!

The participation of students in the co-curricular programme of the institutions too is not active. About 10 per cent of the students take part curricular activities. Ninety per cent of the students....jokers and their only opportunity for self-expression is incognito crowd behaviour. The participation of even the ten per cent is only at a superficial level, The institutions have no arrangements for sustained encouragement and systematic coaching. Most of the students stay out of the system and become easy prey to acts of indiscipline.

Change in the age of marriage too has created a number of problems. While the age of marriage has gone up, the period between sexual maturity and marriage has not been filled by any prospects of gratification or even a closer presence of young women. Our hypothetical student has no girl friend" or wife from whom he would experience a pressure of obligation. There is so little to bind the youth into a pleasing or compelling routine. The sexual vacuum creates so many disturbing situations-there is a mind which cannot attach itself to intellectual objects, a libido which is prevented from attaching itself to sexual objects, a spirit which resents the burden of familial discipline and resists incorporation into modern impersonal adult institution. No wonder, such students take recourse to rebellious acts.

Students from rural areas find very upsetting situations in the colleges and universities in the urban areas. Much of what was formerly certain and stable like one's most cherished and private ideals about oneself are challenged-the fresher changes a lot back and forth; he loses the old foothold and does not easily get the new one because of intense competition all round. Such a student is easily led by clever antisocial elements.

There are quite a big number of students who are not bright enough to be recognised in their academic work and those who do not have leadership qualities, but wish to be recognised, indulge in acts of indiscipline to get attention. Being unruly is the only way in which they can achieve recognition from their fellow students and educational authorities. Some students, particularly from law colleges, are ambitious to become political leaders *(netas)* in their life. They feel that the way to success is to prove themselves as such by organising protests, leading strikes and demonstrations Sitting in *dharnas,* delivering fiery speeches-taking advantage of the inexperienced-they are potential creators of unrest to achieve their selfish goal. Some students lack the ability to succeed in education and thus are unable to satisfy the ambitions of parents. Frustration felt at the home front leads to problems of adjustment. University or college is the easiest target to release their frustration or anxiety

The administration of colleges and universities too is defective. The student is not actively involved in the formation of policy by which he is to be served or administered. No wonder he feels no responsibility at all for the welfare of the institution. His discipline is more indifferent than bad, but distorted by sudden outbursts. His behaviour often lacks form, purpose, clear intention or controlled force. Indiscipline comes as an eruption rather than as effect. Methodology of teaching, instead of being student centered in subject-centered and hence is faulty. There is a variety of students in colleges and universities-rural and urban, those from convent schools and colleges and from ordinary schools and colleges, from upper strata of society and those from scheduled castes,, tribes and backward classes. Methods of teaching are the same for all, no wonder the material grasped varies with individual groups and much of teacher effort goes waste. The disgruntled and frustrated students start indulging in antisocial acts.

Adequate efforts are not made to collect sufficient information about the personal and family background of the students, their daily life-leisure time activities, attitudes, perceptions and aspirations about future, their relationship with the college/university authorities and with the society. There is no arrangement of guidance and counselling in majority of our institutions. There is no one to whom the student may go for help and guidance. He feels lonely and bewildered and can fall an easy prey to antisocial activities.

There is a lurking fear of unemployment among the youth. Even when jobs are available, there is an uneasy feeling that extraneous considerations and not merit alone play a part recruitment. There is a lack of sense of purpose and fulfilment naturally leading to unrest. Sharp break in the medium of instruction secondary schools and colleges and universities is another cause of uneasiness among the students. It leads to low achievement and hence unrest among the students. Standard of films to which students are being constantly exposed is very low. These do not help the students raise their educational and moral standards. Since sex and violence are dominant in films, students like erotic and violent situations in real life also.

The college and university education is mainly theoretical. Education is not practical. 'Earn while you learn' schemes are introduced in very few institutions. The students seldom acquire confidence in the practical vocational courses. Life in the institutions and outside is different. This cleavage also leads to unrest among the students. Gradual erosion of university autonomy is another significant cause leading to student unrest. Frequent government interference in the day-to-day working of several universities has weakened the prestige and authority of their administration. The moral influence which the Vice-Chancellor and other educationists have so far been able to wield with the student community has also received a severe jolt.

Educational programmes, patterns and policies are being dictated by half-baked politicians. The educational authorities are being slighted-teacher's status of yore is no longer there. All this leads to indiscipline.

Sometimes strikes and *dharnas* are engineered by political Parties-they use the objectives. The authorities-both college/university and even the police, are afraid of student power. Students are confident that they will not be met with full vigour by law authorities who first resist, then yield. Authorities are generally halfhearted and undeciding in courting aggression. Every agitation seems to be a success. Thus even serious-minded students join because they feel they will be gainers-always.

Efforts should be made to identify the students' problems, analyse issues, arrive at diagnosis and to adopt immediate and long-term remedies. Rapport should be established with the students. A beginning may be made through the pre and post admission orientation programme. Students should be made aware of both their potentials and the challenges in the formal academic education within the shortest possible time. They should also be acquainted with the methodology of work. This will help create both self-confidence and motivation to carry on education instead of drifting into the jungle of chaos around.

Students should be made responsible for organising their own co-curricular and extra-curricular activities. The sharing of administration will help them in caring for it.

Steps should be taken to encourage teacher-pupil intimacy. Teachers should be recruited not only on the basis of academic distinctions but also of psychological competence for the profession. The emphasis should be placed on the practical rather than the merely theoretical aspects of knowledge. The intention and effort of the educational policy should be to produce quality graduates who can manage various industries-agricultural and animal farms and take up other extension posts. Education imparted in the colleges and universities should be linked more effectively with the employment needs of our developing economy. Special training courses may be started and 'Earn while you learn' schemes introduced. This would not only give the students a chance to apply what they have learnt in the classrooms to situations which they have to face later in life but also enable them to acquire confidence in the know, how they have learnt. Such schemes would also provide the students with much needed financial assistance.

The dichotomy in the media of instruction between the secondary schools, colleges and universities must end at the earliest. This would enable us to release the creative energies of young people. Some positive measures should be taken to involve the from rural areas, backward communities, etc. in educational activities and also provide them with welfare, cultural and sports facilities. In every large institution, there should be a machinery other than the Principal or Vice-Chancellor for sorting out student problems, related with academic achievement, physical facilities, financial assistance, etc. It should be the duty of this organisation to collect optimum information through questionnaires and contact with student leaders and their various organisations throughout the session. It should be possible for such an organisation to more or less foresee student demands and the authorities should have done their own thinking about them, taking into consideration and in confidence all the agencies before the formal charter of demands is prepared and placed before the authorities.

Students should be actively involved in the administration and policy-making agencies. Student participation should be sought, not as an eyewash, but in correspondence with the firm faith that in the changing times decisions are not forced on others but are evolved with their cooperation.

There should be student-faculty dialogue on burning topics like abolition of attendance, admission policy, internal assessment etc., so as to arrive at their joint wisdom. This then can be put before the various university/governmental agencies for consideration and decision. A 24-hour concept of education should be developed. As most significant learning takes place outside the classroom, there should be arrangement for multifarious activities and participation, though voluntary, should be encouraged through incentives.

Student Welfare Committees may be constituted to implement comprehensive student welfare and development programmes. Guidance and Counselling should be made an integral part of every college and university. Standing Committees should be established at the national, state, university and college levels. These committees should be vigilant of all the incidents and developments that occur. They must be fully aware of the campus problems and must be in a position to act even as a grievance committee. Senior students should be the members of such a committee.

We must impress upon our students to fend for themselves. That way, even when they become unruly, they should have something to fall back upon such as say a job of a whole time or part-time nature, after they have let the steam out. We should encourage among our youth the much needed initiative instead of just nose-leading of which we have plenty at the moment. Student services should be made an integral part of every college and university. These services should be keyed to assist young people in the process of growing up and in the development of self-reliance and to learn through guided experiences. The guidance and counselling process should emphasis remediation for those few students who need some assistance with adjustment problems at crisis points in their fives. Various political parties should evolve a code of conduct and build up a convention, that whenever any serious manifestation of student indiscipline takes place, they would join hands to explore cooperatively its causes and possible remedies.

# 4 Techniques

Dunsmoor and Miller are of the view that the core of student counselling is to help the student to help himself. From this point of view they describe the following purposes of student counselling:

1. To give the student information on matters important to success.
2. To get information about student which will be of help in solving his problems.
3. To establish a feeling of mutual understanding between student and teacher.
4. To help the student work out a plan for solving his difficulties.
5. To help the student know himself better-his interests, abilities, aptitudes and opportunities.
6. To encourage and develop special abilities and right attitudes.
7. To inspire successful endeavor toward attainment.
8. To assist the student in planning for educational and vocational choices.

It is obvious that the goal of counselling is problem clarification and self-directed needs. The counselling officer helps the student to understand the problems and helps the student to help himself. In this process, the role or the student is objective self-assessment of the situation and the role of counselling officer is to formulate the decision making process and to act as the stimulator of insights and sensitivities of the student.

Counselling does not solve the problems but helps in solving and if solution is not possible to help face challenges and to live with them.

The fact is so well brought out in Hannah's Greenbook. Here, the girl bitterly accuses her psychiatrist after an unpleasant incident-what good is your reality when justice fails and dishonesty is glossed over and the ones who keep faith suffer—what good is you reality then?

The response is "..I never promised you a rose garden, I never promised you perfect justice...and I never promised you peace or happiness. My help is so that you can be free to fight for all of these things. The only reality I offer is challenge and being well is being free to accept is or not at whatever level you are capable. I never promise lies and the rose garden world of perfection is a lie and a bore too."

In education our goal is guidance; our technique among others is counselling"-has been aptly said by David V. Tiedeman. Counselling is said to be the core of the entire guidance programme. It is considered to be the most intimate and vital part of the guidance programme.

Counselling is as old as society itself. In every day life, we find, counselling goes on at many levels-in a family setup, parents counsel their children, in society doctors counsel patients, lawyers clients, teachers students. In other words, there is no limit to the problems on which counselling can be offered nor to the type of persons who can render this help.

Professional counselling, in its present form, is a recent development. Colleges and universities, industries an business establishments are becoming increasingly interested in counselling and its potential for improving interpersonal relationships. It is believed, where no counsel is, the people fall; but in the multitude of counsellors, there is safety. No wonder, counselling is being recognised as an important technique of guidance here, there are everywhere! Before we discuss the how of his technique, let us try to know what counselling is?

Counselling has been understood and defined in a number of ways:

i. Webster's dictionary defines counselling as "Consultation, mutual interchange of opinions, deliberating together."

ii. Wren says, "Counselling is a dynamic and purposeful relationship between two people who approach to mutually defined problems with mutual consideration of each other to the end that the younger or less mature, or more troubled of the two is aide to a self-determined resolution of his problem."

iii. James Michael Lee and Nathaniel J. Pattan say, "Counselling is the relationship between two persons in which one of them attempts to assist the other in so organising himself as to attain a particular form of happiness, adjustment to a life-situation, or in short, self-actualisation. Counselling always involves a one-to-one relationship, that is one client and one guidance worker in a formal or an informal interview situation."

iv. Merle M. Ohlsen writes, "Counselling is an accepting, trusting an safe relationship in which clients learn to discuss openly what worries and upsets them, to define precise behaviour goals, to acquire the essential social skills, and to develop the courage and self-confidence to implement desired new behaviours."

v. According to Arbuckle, "Counselling is helping a person to come to see who he really is, what he has and does not have; what he can do easily, what he can do with difficulty and what he probably cannot do at all...(It) is a close sharing of a human relationship with one who has form him a high regard; one who can offer him unconditional acceptance, but own who has no guarantees, no answers."

vi. Pepinsky and Pepinsky feel, "Counselling relationship refers to the interaction which (i) occurs between two individual called "counsellor" and "client", (ii) takes place within a professional setting and (iii) is initiated and maintained as a means of facilitating changes in the behaviour of the client. The Counselling relationship develops from the interaction between two individuals, one a professionally trained worker and the other a person who seeks his services."

vii. Hahn and Maclean define "Counselling as a process which takes place in a one-to-one relationship between an individual beset by problems with which he cannot cope alone and a professional worker whose training and experience have qualified him to help others reach solutions to various types of personal difficulties."

viii. Blocker explains it as "helping an individual became aware of himself an the ways in which he is reacting to the behavioural influences of his environment. It further helps him to establish some personal meaning for this behaviour and to develop and clarify a set of goals and values for future behaviour."

An analysis of the above viewpoints will reveal the major elements of counselling.

(a) Counselling involves two individuals-one seeking help and the other, a professionally trained person who can help the first.

(b) There should be a relationship of mutual respect between the two individuals. The counsellor should be friendly and co-operative and the counsellee should have trust and confidence in the counsellor.

(c) The aim of counselling is to help a student to form a decision, make a choice or find a direction at some important fork in the road such as that of planning a life career, a programme in college or university, or a campaign to obtain employment.

(d) It helps the counsellee acquire independence and develop a sense of responsibility. It helps him explore and fully utilise his potentialities and actualise himself.

(e) It is more than advice-giving. Progress comes through the thinking that a person with a problem does for himself rather than through solutions suggested by the counsellors.

(f) It involves something more than the solution to an immediate problem. Its function is to produce changes in the individual that will enable him to extricate himself from his immediate difficulties.

(g) It concerns itself with attitudes as well as action.

(h) Emotional rather than purely intellectual attitudes are the raw material of the counselling process. Information and intellectual understanding have their place in the counselling process. But it is the emotionalized feelings which are most important.

Counselling is a generic service of student personnel work having a wide range of activities and includes faculty advising, counselling in psychological clinics, mental hygiene and other specialised types of counselling. It is a body of techniques which helps young individuals to grow up normally through guided learning. Counselling has proved to be very useful wherever the development of an individual student is cared for. It helps an individual to know himself better, gives him confidence, encourages his self-directiveness and provides him with new vision to grow.

What counselling is not

1. Counselling is not giving information though information may be given.
2. Counselling is not giving advice, making suggestions and recommendations.
3. Counselling is not influencing the client's values, attitudes, beliefs, interests, decisions, etc. with r without any threat or admonition.

The main objective of counselling is to bring about a *voluntary* change in the client. for this purpose, the counsellor provides facilities to help achieve the desired change or make the suitable choice. *The client alone is responsible for the decisions or the choices he make, though that counsellor may assist in this process by his warmth and understanding relationship.*

**Scope of counselling**

Counselling has a vast scope. According to Williamson, "The techniques of counselling individual students may be observed in greatly modified form, in the individualized service; granting loans and scholarships; handling discipline cases; assignment of rooms and selection of room-mates in dormitories; advising on student activities and programmes; helping students choose vocational objectives; selecting optional courses of study; learning to read at college rate and comprehension."

Concerns about educational progress, course programme planning financial and health matters, and problems of family, social and emotional adjustment are commonly expressed in the context of counselling. Very often, many of these are closely intertwined in experience of the same student. In such instances, terms such as 'vocational problem' and 'emotional problem' are nothing more than convenient labels which serve as tentative and approximate methods of classifying counseling cases. It often happens that a problem which is initially expressed by the student as simply one of learning how to study better or of making a suitable vocational choice turns out to be much more complex than that.

**Levels of counselling**

Counselling is a term that is used quite loosely for face-to-face interviews in which the counsellor attempts non-coercively to help the counsellee or client, or a group of clients, to make personal decisions.

It may be helpful to differentiate three levels of activity related to training:

1. *Informal counselling*: It is any helping relationship by responsible person who may have little or no training for the work. For instance, ladies helping patients in hospitals through friendly conversation with them.

2. *Non-Specialist counselling by professionals*: It is the help provided by physicians, lawyers, teachers, ministers, and others who do a great deal of face-to-face work with psychological problems in the course of their other work. Sometimes, special titles are used like "religious counselling" or "financial counselling".

3. *Professional counselling*: It is helping another person with decision and life-plans, whether personal or

educational vocational, by a person specially trained for this work. Professional counsellors are usually psychologists, or educational psychologists. 'Professional' means among other things the possession of master's or doctor's degree with at least a year of supervision by a trained professional and the acceptance of a professional code of ethics. Training for psychologists, among other things, emphasises test interpretation, research, the psychology of personality, occupational information and experience with a variety of clients.

**Classification of counselling**

Counselling can be classified according to the nature of the problem, the complexity of treatment, and the competence of the counsellor. Some writers classify counselling in terms of several factors. Lloyd Jones and Smith, for example, describe various levels of counseling with respect to the depth of the problem, length of contact, degree of need, and the skill of the counsellor.

At the Surface level is the counselling offered when the student wishes only some item of information. The counselling given may be casual; it is brief, and it may be superficial inn that it is not extensive or intensive. The need for help is important even though slight, and the relationship maintained through the brief contact should not be less than that maintained during the long counselling session. Counselling at the next level requires a more prolonged contact because the counsellee needs more and complicated information. He may, for example, wish assistance in planning a programme of study for a two or four year period. As the problems became more complicated and as more intensive study of the case is required, and more specialised help is needed, counselling at deeper levels becomes necessary. When the student is seriously disturbed, therapeutic counselling may be needed. Williamson feels that counselling is needed not only for helping individuals to gain insight into their emotional conflicts but also for helping them with problems stemming from lack of information, such as information about vocational aptitudes and interests or about work opportunities, so that they may conduct their future adjustments in such a way, that 'minimum of maladaptive repressions' occur.

**When counselling is required?**

The following are some of the situations in which counselling is needed:

i. When the student needs not only reliable information but an interested interpretation of such information as meets his own personal difficulties.

ii. When the students needs a wide, sympathetic listener with border experience than his own, to whom he can recount his difficulties and from whom he may gain suggestions regarding his own proposed plan of action.

iii. When the counsellor has access to facilities for helping in the solution of a students' problem to which the student does not have easy access.

iv. When the student is unaware that he has a certain problem but of his best development, must be around to a consciousness of that problem.

v. When the student is aware of a problem and of the strain and difficulty it is causing, but is unable to define and understand it, and is unable to cope with it independently.

**Who should be counselled?**

The following type of students are in urgent need of counselling:

i. Students who have a consistent record of under-achievement.

ii. Students whose scholastic achievement drops suddenly.

iii. Students who need financial aid in order to continue their studies.

iv. Students who find it difficult to participate in class and extra-class activities.

v. Students who use exhibitionism for gaining recognition or attention in class.

vi. Students who find it difficult to adjust to the college/university.

vii. Students who suddenly decide to drop out of college/university.

viii. Students who display unusual ability in any direction intellectual, artistic, musical, etc.

ix. Students who have behaviour problems such as drug addiction, aggressiveness, bullying, stealing, shyness, timidity, etc.

**Different counselling techniques**

There techniques are used for counselling. These are divided on the basis of the n nature of the counselling process an the part of the counsellor.

1. Directive or Prescriptive or Counsellor-centered counselling.

2. Non-directive or Permissive of Client-centered counselling.

3. Eclectic counselling.

**Directive or prescriptive or counsellor-centered counselling:**

E.G. Williamson is the chief exponent of this viewpoint. Such type of counselling involves six essential steps:

— *Analysis*-Collection from a variety of sources the data needed for a adequate understanding of the student.

— *Synthesis-* Summarising and organising the data so that they reveal the students' assets, liabilities, adjustments and maladjustments.

— *Diagnosis-*Formulating conclusions regarding the nature and the cause of the problems exhibited by the student.

— *Prognosis-* Predicting the future development of the student's problems.

— *Counselling-* The counsellor's taking steps with the student to bring about adjustment and readjustment for the student.

— *Follow-up-*Helping the student with new problems or with recurrence of the original problem and determining the effectiveness of the counselling provided to him.

Here the counsellor plays the major role; he does all that he can to get the counsellee to make a decision in keeping with his diagnosis. He tired to direct the thinking of the consellee by informing, explaining, interpreting and advising. A considerably use of interpretations and direction by the counsellor has led to this type of counselling being described as directive or counsellor-centered or active approach technique.

**Non-directive or permissive or client-centered counselling**

Car R. Rogers is the chief exponent of this viewpoint. In this type of counselling, it is the client-the counsellee-who is the pivot. He takes an active part in the process of therapy. He gains insight into his problem with the help of the counsellor. It is he who takes decisions as to the action to be taken. The counsellor's role is passive. This type of counselling is a growth experience. The goal is the independence and integration of the client rather than the solution of particular problem. The principal function of the counsellor is not to cultivate self-understanding in the client but instead, to create an atmosphere in which the client can work out his own understanding. The emotional elements or the feeling aspects are stressed rather than the intellectual aspects and the counselling leads to a voluntary choice of action. In this type of counselling, we make use of few or no diagnostic instruments, except in typical situations when the individual is handicapped due to certain limitations.

**Eclectic counselling**

Some psychologists like Bordin believe that Rogers and Williamson are towards opposite ends of the pole and the counselling methods may be evaluated along a continuum from non-directive to directive. When a counsellor deliberately tries to incorporate in his practice both directive and non-directive techniques, the result is eclecticism. F.C. Thorne, who is the exponent of this view, finds that it is possible for a counsellor to alternate between directive and non-directive methods even in the same interview without disrupting the non-directive permissive relationship with the client. Here, the counsellor first studies the personality and needs of the individual. He then selects the technique that would be most helpful for the individual. He can start with the directive one but when the situation demands, the counsellor may switch over to the non-directive and vice-versa. The attempt is made to adjust the techniques to the requirements of the situation and the individual. Even techniques like reassurance, merely giving information, case history, testing, etc. can be used to achieve the purpose. The counsellor must be competent and proficient in the use of all available methods. The validity of the results is determined by the skill with which any method is used with reference to etiologic diagnosis and the indications of each individual case. The critical factor is not what method is used but rater the skill with which it is used.

The process of eclectic counselling proceeds somewhat along the following lines:

i. Counselling may be preceded by an intake interview.

ii. During the opening phase of counselling, the counsellor tries to establish rapport and may have to do structuring so that the client understands what to expect of counselling.

iii. Often a tentative diagnosis is made which may include the collection of a case history and a plan for counselling is formulated.

iv. To enhance the client's self-understanding, information, about him and his background may be gathered form various sources. The client needs to be helped to assimilate this information.

v. Educational, occupational and social information, if needed by the client, may be supplied to him.

vi. The client achieves emotional release and insights, alters his perceptions and attitudes about himself and his situations.

vii. During the closing phase, the client makes decisions and plans, modifies behaviour, solves his problems.

vii. There may be follow-up contact, if needed.

No matter what method or view-point-directive, non-directive or eclectic is employed in the practice of interviewing and counselling, counselling should have developmental preventive and remedial values. It is obvious that counselling process is viewed differently by different approaches, But in spite of the diversity in approaches to counselling, there are common factors which are:

i. All counsellors accept the importance of ideal counselling relationship.

ii. Interview is the basic tool of counselling.

iii. The counselling relationship is built during interviews.

iv. All counsellors realise the importance of acceptance of and respect for the counsellee.

v. "Honesty", "sincerity", or "Openness" of the counsellor is another common element with all counselling approaches. How the counsellee perceives the counsellor is more important than even the skills and the knowledge of the counsellor.

**Types of counselling**

Counselling can be:

1. Individual, and

2. Group.

***1. Individual counselling tools***

Individual counselling can be done through Interviews of different types.

*(a) Interview*

Interview is a give and take of views between the interviewer and the interviewee. It consists of consultation, mutual interchange of opinions and deliberating together. It can be used to get information, to give information and to change behaviour. Its purpose, thus is three-fold-it involves gathering all available pertinent facts, making a diagnosis on the basis of all the evidence and formulating an appropriate plan of action. All problems may no be settled in the interview but to be successful, it should lead to some plan of action. Its aim should be to serve the individual even though the counsellor may do no more than present the facts in a more objective light, thus enabling the student to see himself, his asses, his liabilities and his opportunities more clearly than he cult see them unaided. The interview may be used for any of several purposes, but a purpose it must have. It may be introductory, fact finding, informative, evaluative, therapeutic in nature and its use for any of these purposes should be clearly recognised by the counselling officer and his subject.

What are some of the specific practical questions which are likely to come up for consideration during an interview? There are a great many such questions of course and they are as varied and as individually coloured as the interviewee who seeks answers them. The student who feels a need to be better informed about his scholastic and vocational prospects may want estimates of his aptitude for college work, his intellectual promise for special fields of training, his disposition to favour or avoid various spheres of activity, and his emotional adjustment tendencies. He may wish to consider with his counsellor the questions as whether he should remain in college, how much additional training he should take, what course he should take and whether he should transfer to another institution. He may decide to ask about the duties and services performed by workers in a particular occupation and about employment requirements and opportunities in that field of work. There might be some difficulties at home or harassment by other students or he might find difficulty in his a adjustment with room-mates in the hostel.

It is obvious there is no simple answer to the question 'what problems should be discussed in an interview?' Perhaps the best rule of thumb is the any personal problem that generally concerns the interviewee or any question that bears upon his personal planning ad decision making activities is a legitimate matter for interview. What is a proper counselling topic for one student may not be suitable for another. There are a number of problems of the students-academic, disciplinary, economic, educational, emotional, residential, social, etc. which necessitate the use of this tool. Here is a suggestive list of problems on which students may seek interview:

Change of subjects
Guidance at bifurcating stage
Courses where available
Courses where available
Co-curricular activities
Free studentship, fee concessions, etc.
Unfair means case
Difficulties at home
Harassment by other students
Misunderstanding with some teachers
Love affair
Prospects after completion of studies
Living in the hostels
How to study?
How to prepare for examinations?

The fact that a student comes to a teacher occasions a meeting and may result into an interview. for some problems , interview may have to be arranged and the interviewee may have to the called for, as stated earlier, under the heading 'Who should be counselled?'

*Types of interviews*

*Introductory interview*

The first interview with a subject should be designed for the purpose of getting mutually acquainted and building rapport, so that follow-up conference and procedures sill be welcomed and appreciated. The counsellor may introduce himself, state the purpose of the interview and advise the subject about the procedures that will be used later. The short ten-to-fifteen minute introductory interview may end with an invitation to the subject to drop in at any time, with making a second appointment, with informing him about the time of the next conference, or with setting the data of the first administration of tests or of any other procedures that are to follow. Expending of whatever time is necessary to establish happy relationship in this introductory interview, is justified. In the part of the counsellee, it involves developing a feeling of ease, born of growing confidence in the counsellors' competence, interest, knowledge, and skill, and a feeling of freedom to reveal both facts and emotions. On the part of the counsellor, it entails treating the student as a responsible adult, being considerate of all attitudes and feelings.

The introductory interview should be held very soon after the students enters the college. If the first interview is delayed until the student runs into difficulty, fails in some subjects, breaks a rule, has trouble with other students or, the like, the counselling officer may not find it easy or possible to establish good relations with the students. The counselling officer should make notes about this introductory interview after the subject has left the conference room. It is not advisable to take or recommend any action on the basis of data obtained in the introductory interview, as there will usually be little information to justify action.

*Fact-finding interviews*

These interviews may be designed to discover the intensity of a counsellee's attitudes towards persons and situations which he cannot or will not reveal in writing or in response to formalised questions which do not allow for indication of strong feelings. Thus interview may reveal interests that had no previously been noted, and it may allow the counsellor to determine their strength and their source. It can be used to obtain information concerning relationships with other persons and about activities that are carried out with them.

*Informative interview*

A counsellee may be interviews for the purpose of informing him about data that have been obtained form other sources, for providing information to answer question that he has raised or of passing on some decision that has been made about him by a person in a position of authority. The counselling officer may also inform a student about such matters as his performance in tests and their interpretation; the acceptance or rejection f an application for a position or for permission to a change in courses, the decision of the principal/head of the department concerning his success in an examination. Many educational-vocational problems of the students are solved by acquisition of new and accurate information about themselves and the world of work or by discovering a different orientation to information which they already possess.

*Therapeutic interviews*

Interview may be used for therapeutic purposes. All of us like to discuss our problems, dreams and aspirations with others in whom we have confidence ad with whom we have rapport. Interview gives a chance to the counsellee to talk about himself, his past, his wishes and fears, his hopes and aspirations. The process of talking things over bring new clarity of thought, relief from over-tension, and a new objectivity. We can know a lot from what the counsellee says, from how he behaves in the interview situation, by noting what the student is not inclined to talk about, what he speaks of with the most satisfaction and the most distress, what are the topics which when mentioned cause him the most embarrassment or inhibition. In other words, it often happens that how a thing is said, seems just as important as what is said and it is only in the interview that this aspect of the counsellee's revelations can be appraised. When through interview the counsellee is permitted to "think aloud" in the presence of a sympathetic listener, it can give a clue to a number of problems of the counsellee.

**Interview procedure**

*1. Preparation*

Interviewing is an art that requires careful planning and preparation for satisfactory performance and good results. Before the interview, the counselling officer needs to work out the entire interview procedure. He needs to be sure as to how is the going to initiate it, what responses are possible to his opening statement, which one of these responses does he want, how he can eliminate the unwanted responses and achieve definite objective.

The following hints can prove useful:

*i. Decide what is to be a accomplished:*

The interviewer knows the problem, when the interviewee comes for the interview, he has his own expectations and objectives. It is, therefore, important for the interviewer to be clear about what is to be accomplished. It will be desirable to write them down.

*ii. Know the interviewee:*

It is necessary to know the interviewee before he comes for the interview. This could be done from college records, test records, cumulative records, activity reports, from his friends and, if necessary, form his parents/ guardians, etc. This will help in two-ways-in giving a good start to the interviewer and in establishing rapport and in solving the problem. Such data can furnish a framework within which the students' problem can be advantageously surveyed.

*iii. Make appointments:*

When appointments are made, both the interviewer and the interviewee are prepared. It saves time.

*iv. Provide for privacy:*
Privacy is an essentials condition of interviewing. It is necessary that the student is in a proper frame of mind induced by privacy and respect for the counseling officer's competence. Interruptions during the course of the interview should not be there.

*v. Practice taking the interviewee's point of view:*
The interviewer must learn to step in the shoes of the interviewee. He must be able to see the interviewee's point of view, how he looks at the problem, how he reacts to the interviewing.

*vi. Know your own personality:*
The interviewer needs to be objective. He must be able to introspect, overcome or at least control his opinions, convictions, attitudes, preconceptions, prejudices, notions, etc.

**The process**

*i. Establish rapport:*
The interviewer should make all out efforts for establishing rapport relationship of confidence, trust and mutual appreciation which helps the counsellee to express himself without inhibitions and resistance. Building of this relationships helped by the atmosphere of the counselling officer's room, his attitude and the initial reception he gives to the counsellee. The room should be attractive and pleasing. The general atmosphere should convey an impression of friendliness and informality. By rising to meet the student as an expected guest, the interviewer may give an impression that he is welcome. By giving him full attention and avoiding a preoccupied manner, he can give to the student the impression that the conference is the most important thing he could be doing at the moment.

*ii. Help the interviewee feel at ease and ready to talk:*
The interviewer should being with topics which are easy to talk about and thus warm up the interviewee. After getting on the main topic, the counselling officer should make the interviewee talk freely. It is essential that the interviewee feels free to express his own ideas unhampered by the ideals, values and preconceptions of the interviewer. He should give advice only sparingly. Even when advice is sought, it would be better to avoid assuming responsibility for the decision which rightly should rest on the student himself.

*iii. At the close of the interview, watch for additional information or new leads in the casual remarks of the interviewee:*
The interviewer should be alert to catch the change of expressions which may drop after the interview has ended when the tension has been released and he is off guard, he may say things which he may have wanted to say earlier but which seemed to him irrelevant or too trivial to mention. The interviewer must always remember that the interview has not yet closed even when he has asked all his questions.

**3. Interpretation**
What the interviewee says is often a mixture of facts, his view of the situation as he sees it, and his feelings. Unless the interviewer has information from other sources, he is often unable to distinguish between fact and fiction. There is another difficulty arising out of the interviewer himself-his tendency to project his ideas and attitudes upon the interviewee. Without interpretation the counsellee may remain on a superficial level of self-understanding. The interpretation to students of the varied aspects of their emotional life is essential and it requires great skill and understanding.

**4. Developing insights and putting them to work**

The process of clarifying and gaining insight naturally leads to the making of decisions and the planning of courses of action. The successful interviewer is resourceful in making the counsellee reach his decisions and put them into practice.

**5. Recording**

There should be an efficient system of recording and maintaining the interview notes. If a complete record is desired, it may ;be necessary to keep a taper-recorder in the room. In cases, where good rapport has been established, the necessary notes can be taken without disturbing the subject. In general, however, the interview will proceed better if no notes are taken. A summary must, however, be written, immediately after the interview, to make sure nothing of importance is forgotten.

**Limitations**

i. The validity of data obtained from interviews is always suspect because the results are contained in judgments made by one person.

ii. The validity and reliability ;of this technique varies with how well and skillfully the interview has been structured and who is conducting it.

iii. Interviewer's bias is another limitation of this technique. Researchers have pointed out the fact that the interviewers report a particular phenomenon according to their own interpretations, understandings, beliefs and attitudes. The validity studies of interviews have revealed very low statistical measures of validity when interview predictions have been compared n the principle of learning. The most important contribution to behavioural counselling has been made by. Pavlov, Skinner, Wolpe and John D. Kumhboltz who believed that neurotic behaviour is acquired and is subject to the established laws of learning.

**Goal**

The goal of behavioural counselling is to change particular behaviour efficiently and specifically.

***The counselling process***

Blackhom and Silverman have suggested the following steps of behavioural counselling:

i *Problem definition*: The counsellor should specifically define the problem-all the circumstances regarding the inappropriate behavivour should be identified.

ii Development and socials history of the problem should be prepared.

iii. *Specification of the Counselling goals*: The client and the counsellor should come to an agreement as to what the problem actually is. It is the counsellor's responsibility to decide if the goal is within his realm of expertise and in accordance with ethical behaviour.

iv *Selection of methods*: The techniques used in the counselling, consistent with the client's goals, need to be selected.

**Techniques of behavioural counselling**

Behaviourists use a variety of techniques to build new habits:

i. *Operant conditioning*: It is based on the idea that a person will learn to behave in a different way if the new behaviour is rewarded and the old behaviour is ignored.

ii. *Aversive conditioning*: It is technique for eliminating specific behaviour patterns. The therapist teaches the person to associate pain and discomfort with the response he wants to unlearn. This form of behaviour therapy has been used successfully to treat alcoholism, homosexuality, obesity and smoking. Dent treated alcoholics by giving them a drug that produces extreme nausea when mixed with alcohol in the stomach. The people were encouraged, infact, instructed to drink, and each time they did they became violently sick. Gradually they began to feel sick everytime they. even saw a bottle of whisky.

*Desensitization*—It is another technique for reducing irrational behaviour. In this technique if a client has described several anxiety producing situations, those situations are ranked from the lowest to the highest in terms of disturbance. The client is instructed in relaxation technique. When this is accomplished each anxious situation is presented starting with the one that produces the least anxiety. As the situation is recalled by the client he is reinforced by the relaxation process until there is no anxiety. Behaviourists have used desensitization to cure phobias about snakes, heights, closed rooms and sex.

*Reciprocal Inhibition*—There are individuals who feel anxious and unhappy most of the time. Wolpe feels behaviourists can treat diffused anxiety. Here the therapist establishes a hierarchy, from the least to the most anxiety, provoking situations. Next he teachers the client to clear his mind, release tense muscles and relax. In some cases, he may use drugs or mild hypnosis to produce relaxation. Once the client has mastered the technique of deep relaxation, they begin at the bottom of his anxiety hierarchy. The therapist asks the person to imagine the least threatening scene and to signals when he begins to feel tense. At the signal, the therapist tells him to forget the scene and concentrate on relaxing. After a short period, he instructs him to return to the scene. This process is repeated until the person feels completely relaxed. Gradually they move up the list until the client is able to imagine the situation he most learn to inhibit anxiety responses with incompatible, deep muscle relaxation. It is obvious that the success of behavioural counselling depends upon the following:

i. establishing a valid hierarchy by ;the client and the therapist;

ii. discovering and adequate reinforcer (cooperant conditioning) by the therapist; and

iii. lack of counter conditioning outside the therapy sessions.

Some psychologists are critical of behavioural counselling. They feel that by concentrating only on behaviour, it presents an over-simplified version of human psychology. These psychologists feel that an individual's mental behaviour is just as important in therapy as his overt behaviour. It is also felt that the behavioural counselling is symptom oriented. Effort is made to smother the neurotic symptoms, no effort is made to remove the conflict that caused them. There is always a danger of the client relapsing intuit to be educated about invite each student for an individual counselling interview, particularly so in case of freshmen, as TDC I year and MA/MSc First year students, who besides their educational and vocational problems, have their peculiar problems of personal and social adjustment as they are passing through the difficult and social adjustment as they are passing through the difficult phase of adolescence. What technique of counselling-directive or non-directive or a combination of both-would be suitable under our cultural set-up is a point that deserves careful consideration at the hands of counselling officers.

**Group guidance**

Group guidance is an important part of the guidance

programme. It is true that the most important objectives in the guidance process are to help the individual achieve selfdirection, self-knowledge and self-realisation-these objectives cannot be achieved in a cultural vacuum. Many important experiences must take place in a group setting, since it is the only way they can be learned realistically.

Group guidance is that relationship in which a guidance worker attempts to assist a number of students to attain for themselves satisfactory development or adjustment to their respective individual or collective life situations. It occurs in a setting in which one or more guidance workers encounter students as a group. Group are best suited for discussing educational and vocational plans, problems relating to adjustment to college and social situations, problems relating to choice of options and choosing a career, economic and occupational problems, personality adjustment problems, etc.

A number of techniques can be used for imparting group guidance:

i. *Informal Discussions* - Informal discussions, if done under the able and skillful leaders, can prove very helpful. These discussions should centre around desirable objectives and should be so guided as to result in conclusions that may be helpful to he group as whole.

ii. *Group Reports* - If the students are divided into groups which have certain specific problems to tackle and later these reports are presented in larger groups. They can help all the members of the group in gaining awareness of a number of problems and their solution.

iii. *Lectures* - Lectures delivered by experts on certain problems too can impart group guidance in an effective way.

iv. *Dramatics* This is another good techniqued of group guidance. If certain interesting topics are dramatised, the students can be given guidance in an interesting way. How to appear for an interview, how to prepare for an examination, how to prepare notes-all these can be dramatised land guidelines suggested to the students in an interesting way.

v. *Question box* - "Question - box" says Jones, "If carefully organised and not too frequently used, is also a desirable technique, for it gives the shy and retiring pupil and opportunity to propose a question that is bothering him without revealing that it is his question". Most of the times, we find the shy student remains buried with his problems as he is not vocal. It is also possible that there are quite a few students having the same problem. So if the question could be proposed in a silent way, the same could be discussed in a group and valuable guidance provided to the students.

vi. *The case conference-* Here the problem faced by the majority of the group is stated concretely by way of a case. Each member of the group reviews his own experience in a similar situation. The group is guided away from the more immediate and temporary advantages to be gained toward more remote and temporary values. Then the effect of the exceptions may be discussed. Some other conditions that should be considered in deciding a plan of action are also gone through. Some generalisations are also formulated which may prove helpful another situations. According to Jones, the entire process of the case conference is an experience in social thinking and it has positive and unique values in the group guidance program.

# 5 Counselling Profession

The control of preparation and practice are two further factors that help define a profession. Through establishing admissions standards for preparation programs and specifying what these programs should accomplish, the guidance profession does exercise some control. But the role of the profession is largely advisory, its recommendations have considerable influence but do not set the standards for all employers. A fifth characteristic of professional identity is personal autonomy in the provision of service, the individual counsellor exercises independent judgement, makes decision, and provides help. Counsellors may have considerable freedom in the way they practice their profession, but little control over allotment of time for specific activities. Even so, there is adequate autonomy for the councillor to utilize professional expertise. A final professional characteristic involves the function of service to others. Counseling and guidance qualify as a profession by this criterion more fully than by any other. There is room for improvement in the applications of standards for preparation and practice; but professional status is justified in all crucial respects.

The American Personnel and Guidance Association has taken the lead in formulating standards for preparation for guidance at the elementary and secondary levels. The guidelines are clear-cut, specific, and constitute excellent models. The secondary school standards have been more extensively studied, reviewed, and developed than those for the elementary school, but the current guides cover all councillors regardless of educational level. Before the most recent standards were adopted in 1973, an earlier set of guidelines had been widely used by counsellor-education institutions and accrediting organizations for self-study and program improvement. A manual was also prepared to help councillor education staffs prepare for evaluations. The new revision brings together existing guide lines for all levels in a unified and comprehensive report. The Association for Counsellor Education and Supervision carries on the development of standards as a continuous process; new revisions will be forthcoming. The introduction to the new standards reflects many contemporary trends. First, it spells out the need for students to demonstrate competencies. Second, it assumes differential rates of student progress; some may take longer to acquire proficiency than other. Third, it considers various models that extend graduate preparation beyond a single year; one such program, for example, combines an undergraduate major in guidance with a year of graduate study.

The four major sections cover objectives; the program of studies and supervised experience; responsibilities concerning students in the program; and support for the counsellor-education program, administrative relations, and institutional resources. The opening section on objectives sets the stage for the program. The major emphases are on explicit, cooperatively planned objectives evolving from input of those involved-counsellor educators, students, and practitioners. Objectives show sensitivity to needs, problems, and trends in schools; they are regularly revised and updated.

The program of studies calls for academic and practical work to enable students to move to increasing levels of competence and responsibility. There are opportunities for observation and involvement in guidance. Responsibility for working face-to-face with individuals and groups comes as competence is developed. Along with increasing competence in helping activities, the program fosters a spirit of inquiry, ethical sensitivity, and skill in self-evaluation. The practical-work component is given specific emphasis; in a one-year period, 60 hours should be spent in face-to-face individual or group work. The third section deals with selection, retention, endorsement, and placement of students. It speaks to student rights, pointing out the need for making clear the criteria and procedures for admitting students, and retaining or separating them from the program. It also indicates the program's responsibility for endorsing and placing graduating students.

The final section covers institutional support for programs in guidance. Emphasis is on cooperative relationships with other college or university departments for courses, and with school settings for practical experience. It specifies a minimum full-time staff of three members and spells out the necessary professional qualifications for those working with students. These standards, which describe what the program should provide and define the professional competencies to be mastered, are of great significance to the beginning students. The APGA standards require preparation to cover all levels of the profession, added emphasis on specialized work settings is to be provided through courses and practical work. For example, students preparing for elementary school counseling would concentrate particularly on courses and practical work designed for this educational level. Preparation for career guidance and participation in career education would feature added emphasis on these areas.

Current standards are oriented to competency, as are several contemporary preparation models. The system-based approach and HRD, for example, emphasize specific competencies, systematic means of achieving them, and evaluation in terms of counsellor effect on counselees. The ACES standards emphasize that programs are to be evaluated in terms of competencies of each student. Such competencies would be illustrated by specific items such as supervised practice in working with groups. Zifferblatt discusses the systems approach, in which specific skills are learned recycled until they reach an acceptable level of competency. Another illustration shows specific and measurable characteristics of many competency approaches in terms of the student's growing self-awareness:

> Given two hours with a group of fellow trainees, the trainee must be able to make five self-observation responses, the validity of which can be confirmed by a majority of group members.

Among other strategies recommended in preparing counsellors is an experiencing-growing-sharing process between counsellor educators and students, which stresses individual development. There is certainly no dearth of models and Santoro, which is a very positive sign. The future of those now in use, however, is not clear. Kennedy described problems that could cause the competency model to fade from the educational scene; it may not be feasible, for example, to keep students in the program until competencies are mastered. Programs must, despite limited resources, prepare counsellors to meet new demands for services and demonstrate effectiveness.

**Legal status, certification, and licensing**

These areas are among the must controversial and ambiguous in the counseling profession; they are of major concern to anyone planning to enter the field.

Potential legal problems revolve around malpractice, right to privacy, serving as defendant tin criminal action, encouraging an illegal act, or involvement in civil disobedience. Certification poses fewer potential problems. Your program will probably meet requirements, but you should known not only the standards in your own state, but also those of any other state you may wish to move to. Licensure is of recent concern. Previously it was critical only for counsellors in some nonschool settings, but it is now emerging as an issue for school counsellors too. Currently the employees of an educational instruction are given sanctions to practice by virtue of their employment status; the institution authorizes their activity and assumes responsibility for performance. This may not be true in the future.

*Legal status:* An understanding of legal factors in essential both for day-to-day practice in conventional types of service, and for anticipating problems that may arise with changing conditions. For example a counsellor may feel existing laws and regulations are harmful and ought to be challenged but must know the consequences of disregarding them and share this information with others who might need to know, particularly pupils. The processes one chooses to bring about changes are to some extent a function of one's political convictions. Counsellors are entitled to their own views, but there are harsh realities to consider when changes involve committing illegal acts. Counseling today has no specific legal status. It has only recently come to be recognized as a formal part of school programs. Few court cases have dealt directly with school counseling, and even fewer statutes specify legal obligations and responsibilities. The status of counsellors must be clarified in the light of the few existing cases and statutes, and on the application of the law to people in general. Enough data are available to spell out some guidelines and to alert counsellor to their responsibilities and limitations. Increasing professionalizing has generated rising concern about legal issues. Counseling today amounts to a service of therapeutic intervention ant he pupils' lives. With the responsibility this implies, it is sometimes uncertain just how the counsellor can offer most help to the counselee without violating civil and criminal law. As Burgum ad Anderson point out, counsellors have no general immunity from criminal law and are subject to civil law. Moreover, while statutes give some general guidelines, state and local laws vary enormously. These are some of the questions a practicing counsellor might encounter on a perfectly routine day: Can I assure the counselee of confidentiality? How about in group work" Can I be held liable for malpractice? Am I likely to become involved in a civil suite for carrying out my assigned responsibilities? Are there counseling activities that might lead to criminal charges?

Questions about confidentiality are the most frequent of all. Can counsellors assure counselees of confidentiality? Except in a state that has privileged communication statutes, the answer is no. Some states do have such statues, but policies are hedged with restrictions. There is no general privileged communication for counsellors, although Burgum and Anderson suggest the federal courts could extend it to them through interpretations of rules of evidence. Regardless of national statutes, however, state and local precedents should be examined before assuring counselees of confidentiality. When the counsellor has determined these legal limits, they should be explained to the counselee. In general, these principle are helpful.

1. If the counselee is a clear danger to self or others, the counsellor cannot maintain confidentiality. Steps should be taken to protect others if they are in danger.

2. Generally the counsellor respects the rights of others to confidentiality.
3. If a counselee is the victim of a crime, there is no privileged communication.
4. School counsellors in most states do not have privileged communication. Where they do, laws may over only certain types of information.
5. For school use the term "privileged communication" can be defined as information shared with the counsellor by the counselee, which the counsellor cannot release without the approval of the counselee.
6. An individual may subpoena personal case material in college files for use in other actions. In the Bates College case, for example, the court upheld the plaintiff's request to view information he though was hampering his admission to other colleges. The more recent Buckley Amendment deals more completely with the question of access to records.

The counsellor must also be concerned with the right to talk to others about the counselee without danger of legal action for libel and slander. Usually if the counsellor makes comments about pupils, sends reports to parents, etc., believing the reports to be true, acting without malicious intent, and communicating only with individuals entitled to such information, legal action for libel and slander would not be successful. Civil liability was an issue infrequently raised in past years, but it is a problem causing concern today. There is no sure way to judge what could be construed as counsellor malpractice. If, however, the counsellor follows the ethics and standards of the profession, malpractice liability would likely not be incurred, even if counseling has not been successful. A key requirement is that the counsellor makes a referral when a problem becomes too difficult to handle. Group counseling involves the same responsibility, except that the probability of malpractice increases-there are more counsellees to observe and understand. Some problems are more likely than others to raise the civil-liability issue, particularly those involving sexual relations and abortion. According to Burgum and Anderson, advice about abortions, including possible medical and psychological complications, are beyond the counsellor's competency. Even so, counsellors must deal with these problems every day. The case of Bogust V. Iverson illustrates the extent to the counsellor's liability. A counsellor in Wisconsin worked with a girl, Jane Dunn, on career, educational, and personal problems for a period of six months. When he felt that she had made all the progress she could, he terminated the case. Six months later, she committed suicide. Her parents sued the counsellor, but the court ruled that he was not liable for failure to inform parents of her condition, and in fact, his training did not make him competent to make a judgement about danger to herself. The six months interval also weighed against placing liability on the counsellor. If the counsellee had become emotionally very upset at the termination of counseling, very likely the counsellor would have been held liable.

With respect to libel, slander, and other area of possible civil liability, the counsellor has no special privilege. It is true that the counsellor can talk or write about a counsellee to those who are entitled to the information without liability for legal action. But giving information to those who are not entitled to it, or doing so with harmful intentions, could result in a defamation suit. The same principles apply to student records; the safest course of action is to include only factual information. Unversified damaging information may make one liable for a civil suit. Since parents can examine records, control release of information, and challenge the contents, civil liability can easily be incurred. Professionally, though not legally, it is the counsellor's responsibility to make sure that all school personnel understand the meaning and use of data. Although it is unlikely, a counsellor can, with the best of intentions, become a defendant in a criminal case. Burgum and Anderson list four possible types of charges:

— Accessory to a crime after the fact

— Encouraging an illegal abortion

— Coconspirator in civil disobedience

— Contributing to the delinquency of a minor

Reading their discussions of each of these situations will add depth to your understanding of guidelines for practice. Burgum and Anderson also describe an illustrative case relating to criminal liability in which the school counsellor, who has developed a good relationship with a boy in the custody of the iuvenile court, inadvertently helped him avoid arrest. The boy, with two companions, robbed a service station and then, realizing the gravity of his actions, went to the counsellor for help. The counsellor convinced the boy that he should turn himself, in but it was late at night, and they agreed he would go to the police the following day. Meanwhile, however, the counsellor committed a series of acts that could make him guilty of being an accessory to a felony. He denied to police that the boy was sin his house. He gave the boy money, which was found in the youth's possession when he tried to skip town the next morning rather than reporting to the police. The counsellor would have been well advised to report the matter to the boy's juvenile office, which would have been in his favour in a trial.

Another area of local concern to the counsellor relates

to the rights of pupils. The Gault case brought about full guarantees of due process for minors. Counsellors can help pupils by making them aware of their legal right to due process in education, free speech, and property ownership. Rights of the handicapped are emphasized by due process provisions of PL 94-142. As Nasman points out, due process is not satisfied by establishing a standard procedure including such steps as informing the individual of charges and providing for a hearing, but rather it demands protection of pupils' right under the Constitution, just as if they were adults involved in legal charges. Due process should fit the situation and protect the pupil from arbitrary, unfair, and autocratic rules and policies. The Buckley Amendment, already mentioned, deserves special attention. This law restricts the use of information in personal records; enforcement involves the denial of federal funds if violations are allowed to occur. In the past, school records were not treated with respect for the individual's rights of privacy, nor have parents and pupils has access to most of the information contained in them. The Buckley Amendment has given parents and pupils of legal age the right to inspect records, including letters, comments, and recommendations. Besides opening up records to pupils and parents, the law restricts access of others to these data. In general, parents must give consent for information in records to be released. Nasman discusses the regulations in detail. The complete law appears in the *APGA Ethical Standards Casebook*. Parts of the Buckley Amendment with specific applicability to counsellors' use of student records are as follows:

> Each educational agency or institution except as may be provided by 99.12 shall permit the parent of a student or an eligible student who is or has been in attendance at the agency or institution, to inspect and review the education records of the student.

> The parent of a student or an eligible student who believes the information contained in the education record of the student is inaccurate or misleading or violates the privacy or other rights of the student may request that the educational agency or institution which maintains the records amend them.

The legal status of counseling is being established through new laws, statutes, and court decisions. While relatively few cases directly affecting counseling have gone through the courts, more can be expected as counseling achieves greater status and visibility as a helping service.

*Certification*: All states regulate the practice of counseling through certification, licensing, or endorsement on a teaching certificate. Certification requirements of counsellors in different states are more striking for uniqueness than for similarity, and certification standards are changing both in scope and nature. The most innovative development is the competency-based program. Dudley and Ruff's survey included only one suggestion of this approach, and only one program of this type was reported in the literature. Now 50 percent of the states have, or are planning a competency-based program, while only about 7 percent are not considering it. Over two thirds of the counsellor preparation programs intent to convert to this approach, even though only about 7 percent have actually done so. The Washington program started in 1971 is an example. Behavioural objectives were established through input of teachers, pupils, administrators, and counsellors. Counsellors have been certified at three levels of competency: preparation, initial, and continuing. The initial-level competencies are the type developed in a masters-level program. Six areas of competency are specified; major ones are counseling, information service, and placement. Deficiencies in any of the competencies must be remedied according to procedures spelled out in guidelines of the certification program.

Program accreditation is closely related to certification of individuals; it also gives students an important indication of the quality of a program and enhances job-getting potential If evaluation for accreditation is performed, it conforms to the counsellor preparation standards already discussed. Shertzer and Stone envision a national system of accreditation by an organization such as the Association for Counsellor Education and Supervision or an educational accrediting agency such as NCATE. There is no national accrediting system in operation today, but there are indications that one may eventually be established.

*Licensure*: This topic is relatively new for counselors, although psychologists have been active in formulating state licensure policies for at least two decades. School counselors have been concerned mainly with certification and have only recently become aware of the potential importance for their work of developments in licensure.

There are important differences between certification and licensure. Each provides a service to the users of counseling by indicating the adequacy of practitioners. Certification laws regulate the use of the title "counsellor" and specify the amount and type of training required for practice. Licensing goes beyond regulating the use of the title and indicates the unique services and practices that fall in the domain of the profession. The term "credentials" is often confused with certification. "Credentials" refers to the degree to other certificate the individual has been awarded; the term is also used to indicate competence for a job. Up to new, licensure has been a concern of counselors in community settings such as mental health agencies and private practice. To date only one state requires licensing for personnel and guidance workers. But recent licensure laws have alerted counselors to the potential for state regulation of some or all of their work. In Ohio, for example, licensing laws on the practice of psychology have been interpreted to limit the use of tests by a counsellor in off-duty hours. In the case, City of Cleveland v. Cook 1975, a counsellor who was not a licensed psychologist was arrested for testing. The court found in favour of the defendant; Ohio counselors are contesting this interpretation of the law. The APGA Model Licensing Law specified the points favoured by he counseling profession, including exemptions for those employed as school counselors. But as the situation now stands, school counselors who plan to enter private practice in states with this type of regulation come under the licensing laws for psychologists. The implications, however, may of far beyond off-duty activities or future career plans. As Sweeney and Sturdevant point out, the Ohio law and other similar ones specify that helping by licensing. Besides, licensure and privileged communication give school psychologists more freedom and prestige than school counselors. Sweeney and Sturdevant see "the right for school counselors to practice at all as being challenged".

Only one state actually licenses counselors, and most experts do not predict that other states will soon follow suit. But the situation may change; both the American Psychological Association and the American Personnel and Guidance Association are actively promoting licensing laws. If counsellors do not establish their own licensing criteria and procedures, others will do it form them. The American Personnel and licensing boards and that licensing requirements are designed for counselors.

Licensure gives every indication of becoming a major issue. Congress and federal agencies are showing increasing interest in occupational sensing. Present methods of licensure testing can be unfair to qualified persons, some, for example, do not perform well on standardized tests. Licensure can affect employment opportunities, status, and legal bases of counseling. Effective and well-designed licensure laws can enhance the counseling profession, project the public, and open up new work opportunities, restrictive and unfair ones will interfere with the contributions of many potentially well qualified to offer others assistance. Sweeney ad Sturdeant and Cottingham recommend that counselors keep up with what is happening in licensure and support favourable alternatives. Their advice points out a responsibility of all members of the profession.

One mark of a profession is a code of ethics. It serves as a guide for providing services and ensures legality in carrying out these services. The counseling profession has a comprehensive, well-developed code, as well as special guidelines for work in schools.

The main points of the section on measurement and evaluation are that the counsellor should understand tests, be particularly cautious about their applicability or minority groups, and present or interpret results in keeping with test validity. The section on ethical standards for research and publishing identified the welfare of the individual as the primary factor to be considered; the counsellor should make every effort to avoid harmful effects of research and should take action to reduce or eliminate such effects if they occur.

The section on consulting and private practice deals more with the activities of the private consultant, although much of the counselor's work with teachers administrators, and parents would be based on consultation principles. The section on personnel administration covers organizational and administrative responsibilities in the school counselor's work setting, particularly the need to establish mutually agreed upon goals with administration for major aspects of the job.

The final section deals with preparation standards and their importance to the beginning student.

The school counselor code of ethics is uniquely helpful for the elementary and secondary level in that it identified responsibilities to self and those with whom the counselor works-pupils, parents, faculty, staff, the school, and the community. In all relations the counsellor respects pupils' dignity, individuality, and right to self-direction. Responsibilities to pupils and parents follow the APGA ethical standards closely, but those relating to staff, community, self, and profession give additional guidelines for cooperative work with colleagues and community agencies, for self-development, and for implementing a contributing role in the profession. In the experience that follow problems are presented for discussion and solutions. Additional examples may be drawn from personal experience and from the casebooks already listed.

**Organizations**

Professional organizations provide counselors with support, facilitate professional development, bring together colleagues with similar interests, offer opportunities for active participation in leadership roles, and provide placement services. Counselors can help themselves by building a strong organization. Representatives of the profession are active at national, state, and local levels to promote favourable legislation and to obtain funds for improved services. Participation can begin during preservice preparation. The American Personnel and Guidance Association, a federation of thirteen divisions, is the most important and best-known organization for counselors. APGA offers student memberships at reduced rates, and students can attend APGA national conventions and take part in programs.

The American School Counselor Association is the

APGA division for school counselors, but others too relate directly to work in public educational settings. These are: National Vocational Guidance Association; Association for Humanistic Education and Development; Association for Measurement and Evaluation in Guidance; Association for Non-White Concerns in Personnel and Guidance; Association for Specialists in Group Work; National Catholic Guidance Conference; and an affiliate, International Association of Counseling Services. The five remaining division deal with particular work settings such as college, university, ad employment service.

APGA and each of its division publish newsletters and journals covering current developments in the field, research, practices, legislation, and sources of information and materials. *Personnel and Guidance of journal* and the newsletter Guidepost are distributed to all APGA members. The American School Counselor Association is the only division that publishes two journals, The School counselor and Elementary School Guidance and Counseling, in addition to a newsletter.

Many other useful materials are available from APGA. Program abstracts, published at the time of the national convention, give summaries of presentations. Educational aids ranging from brochures, reprint series, and books to cassettes and films, may be obtained at reasonable cost. APGA publications include Hosford and de Visser's book Behavioural Approaches to Counseling ad an accompanying series of eight films keyed to units in the book. The organization also offers a seven-unit interviewing and communication skills development program, Influencing Human Interaction, which includes films, cassette tapes, filmstrips, and books.

Students and counselors alike can participate in APGA by contributing to its many professional journals. Editors urge members who have something to say to submit material for publication. Journal staff members give helpful and detailed advice on how to prepare articles for publication, explain common faults that result in rejections, and describe the step-by-step process of editing and publishing a professional journal. Articles that pass the editor are given blind reviews, and evaluators' comments are passed on to the author. At regular intervals each journal prints guidelines for authors specifying length, format number of copies of manuscripts to be submitted, and other such details.

*Collective bargaining*: Counselors, like their teaching colleagues, are using collective bargaining, to obtain better salaries, improved working conditions, and other benefits. Humes and Kennedy view the process as a means to gain a power base for achieving professional status in the school ad a full voice in decision making. Creange believes that building a strong, broad-based national organization is one of the most critical issues facing school counseling today. But the American School Counselor Association has found little interest among counselors in collective negotiation. Many counselors are concerned with the question of professionalism v. collective negotiations; thus there is a search for a strong organizational base to advance the status of the profession, to protect job security, and to ensure a voice in determining professional roles and responsibilities.

**Colleagues in non-school settings**

Counselors are employed in educational institutions, community agencies, business and industry, hospitals, and clinics. In their comprehensive monograph on employment opportunities, careers in Counseling ad Guidance, Stone and Shertzer identify eighteen settings: vocational and technical schools; community and junior colleges; colleges and universities; vocational rehabilitation; U.S. Employment Service; Veterans Administration; programs for the disadvantaged;

correctional and penal institutions; community mental health clinics; family service agencies; child-guidance clinics; Hewish Vocational Service; Urban League,; marriage counseling; business and industry; adult education; pastoral counseling; and private practice. The divisions of APGA identify settings other than public schools such as colleges and universities; rehabilitation services; employment services; and correctional and penal settings. Another listing of opportunities in the counseling profession includes business and industry; employment; and higher education. The these could be added counseling older persons, and a variety of services in consulting firms.

These lists show mixtures of settings, programs, and specialties. This reflects the situation with actual job opportunities; counselling older persons, for example, may be done in çolleges, businesses, and community settings,. In each setting, however, the basic competencies, ethical standards, and legal guidelines apply. Priorities vary, however. There may, for example, be more responsibility in one setting for face-to-face work, while in another higher priority goes to coordination services. The focus of the work may also differ; career and program planning may consume most of the counselor's time in one institution, while in another personal therapeutic help may be the major emphasis.

Counseling takes on somewhat different forms in such post-high-school educational settings as voc-tech centers, community and junior colleges, and four-year colleges and universities. In vocational and technical centers emphasis is typically on career planning and placement; the master's degree may be adequate qualification. The role and function statement for the voc-tech setting resembles the statement for the high school. Community and junior-college counseling more closely resembles counseling at the college and university levels. Emphasis is developmental, but career planning and placement are particularly important for students in terminal occupational-preparation programs. The work of community-college counselors ranges from therapeutic and developmental programs to programs emphasizing career guidance, counseling, placement, testing, and a variety of administrative duties.

The college and university level typically offers two major types of work roles-one in the counseling-center setting, the other in general student personnel. The counseling center provides individual and group counseling and is moving toward functions of influencing student life and intervening in the campus community. Placement offices, which in the past have emphasized interviews with prospective employers for graduating students, are now becoming involved in career development and guidance and may offer services to entering students. Student-personnel work is putting increasing emphasis on student development, establishing living-learning centers on campus, and outreach and consultation, and counselors are finding new areas to apply their skills and expertise.

Community agencies and services offer a wide variety of occupational opportunities for counselors. Interest in these settings and private practice is reflected in the increasing concern about licensure. Counselors work in community mental-health agencies, family-service agencies, crisis-intervention centers, halfway houses, drug-counseling centers, and a host of programmes set up for special populations, such as minorities, the disadvantaged, and the unemployed. Each of these services typically involves some counseling, particularly those that deal with interpersonal conflicts and emotional problems. Those for work problems may put more emphasis on placement and training.

Working with older persons is one of the major new opportunities for counselors. The need is apparent. Few services exist. Counselor-preparation programs have done very litter to develop competencies, but interest is increasing. The reasons for growing concern are not difficult to understand. IT is predicted that by the year 2000 one half of the U.S. population will be over 50 years of age and one third will be over 65. Also, there is increasing emphasis on providing counseling over the entire life span. The Federal-State Employment Service is one of the largest employers of counselors in the country. Under the Comprehensive Employment and Training Act of 1973, many special programs for guidance and training were taken out of the Employment Service, but its major function has not changed. There is a trend to provide more counseling to job seekers and to upgrade the qualifications of counselors. The CETA program emphasizes placement for work and/or training, and thus is mainly concerned in helping individuals to understand their abilities and interests and to make decisions. Rehabilitation counselors offer assistance to a wide range of handicapped individuals. Typically the master's degree is required. Work is making increasing use of a counseling approach rather than job finding and physical restoration, and its major aim is to increase the effectiveness of rehabilitation and job placement. Preparation is comparable to a school counsellors, with the addition of courses on medical aspects of disability, rehabilitation procedures, and agencies. Since the major emphasis is to get the handicapped individual into a suitable job or preparation program, the assessment of potential through tests and medical examinations is a major function. In helping the handicapped individual move into the new setting successfully, the counselor must know a great deal about environments and utilize counseling to deal with attitudes that could interfere with success.

Opportunities for counselors are also growing in correctional settings. Penal institutions offer jobs in which counselors serve as links to the community, and work with delinquents. This setting has expanded enough in recent years to merit a special feature section in the Personal and Guidance Journal and the establishing of a separate APGA division. Programs aimed at upgrading the skills of correctional staffs make use of counseling methods and offer a new consultation-training role for counselors in the correctional setting. In this approach, counselors use group methods to help correctional officers learn more effective ways to deal with inmates.

### The personnel for counselling programmes

Teamwork is a popular American concept that appears to have been originally and still is prevalently associated with athletic teams. Coaches and sportswriters consistently extol the virtues of the cooperative enterprise known as teamwork. Even though individual stars are clearly identifiable in most team sports, they are always quick to acknowledge the contributions of their teammates to their stardom and the interdependence that each member of the team has on the others in the pursuit of their mutual goals. This harmonious working together to accomplish a mutual goal is also noticeable in such cooperative endeavors as musical groups, surgical team, army tank crews, and aircraft crews. One could almost conclude that we have become a nation of "teams" as recent generations have seen the concept of teamwork expanded to encompass many organizations as well as institutional and agency settings. It is no longer uncommon, for example, to hear industrial leaders talk about the labour management team or the school principal to commend his or her educational team or a community agency to refer to its psychological team. Regardless of the fact that the terminology may be overworked at times, we must accept the concept of teamwork as an important one if we are to efficiently and effectively bring all the potential resources of the psychological community to bear on behalf of its clients. In advocating a "team" concept we note the following.

- Teams are composed of individuals who are bound together in the pursuit of a common goal. This pursuit is enhanced by their functioning together as a unit. Teams are most effective when members of the team learn mutually complementary roles in order that duplication, overlapping, and competitive activities may be minimized.
- Working together, sharing knowledge and teamwork, when feasible, permits each to use his or her unique talents while determining who will perform the shared talents
- There is no single "best" team system or pattern of team organization; rather, many variations may be anticipated, since a team presumes the best available combination of personnel for the task at hand. For example, some teams may include both community and school personnel, faculty and student representatives, and/or professionals and paraprofessionals.
- The counselor, as well as other professional helpers, may have a variety of roles and may be a member of a variety of "teams" within a specific setting. We recognize that the number and variety of these roles will vary from setting to setting, as on some teams, for example, the counselor will be expected to function as a leader, whereas on others, he or she will function as a follower. Like the skilled magician or juggler, she or he must be adept in "wearing the hat" most appropriate to the

immediate activity in which she or he is engaged.

**The professional helping team for schools**

The school counseling program is an integral part-an important "team" in the total educational enterprise. Whereas this very fact is one of the potential strengths of the program, since by implication everyone is thus involved, it is also at the same time, a complicating factor. If, in fact, everyone is involved, then roles and relationships must be clarified to the point that each recognizes not only his or her own role and function but also that of colleagues in the total counseling and educational effort. Thus, whereas the team concept for schools has long suggested that the school counselor, teacher, administrator, and other personnel specialists must work together to accomplish the objectives of the school counseling and guidance program, one of the perennial problems which countless studies have enumerated has been the failure to clearly define, in both theory and practice, roles and relationships in such programs. Another contributing factor that must be taken into consideration is the continuous call for educational change and innovation which threatens to obliterate many of the traditional structures and roles within education. Thus, at a time when many counselors are still trying to clearly identify their roles and relationships within the educational framework as viewed traditionally, change are taking place that may very well make this attempt to specify roles in terms of job descriptions, it is more appropriate to examine the special contribution each member of the "team" may be reasonably expected to make.

**The school counselors' special contributions**

The school counselor is obviously the central figure on the educational guidance team, for she or he is the specialist who brings unique knowledge and skills to the program without which it could not function. More specially, the counselor is frequently the only professional in the school setting prepared to offer individual and group counseling to students, parents, and teacher. The councelor also posses special knowledge in the area of educational and career development and adjustment, future planning and placement needs.

In addition to these traditional skills and knowledge, school counselors have, in recent years, played increasingly significant roles as consultants to other adults both within and without the educational setting who are also concerned with the pupil's well-being and development. Counselors will recognize that on many occasions they will be more effective when working through and with other significant adults in the individual pupils' life, such as parents, other educators, ministers, and youth workers. This consultation involvement with parents, teachers, and other adults is receiving greater attention as "writers within the counseling profession indicate that all school counselors must conceptualize pupils not as isolated individuals but as members of systems; i.e., family systems, learning systems, and community systems.

> Several reasons can also be stated for the school counselor's choosing to use the school setting for increased involvement and counseling with family systems. First, many personality theories support the idea that family environment and child-rearing practices influence the developing individual. Second, there has been increased acceptance of the school's becoming more involved with the home environment. Third, schools are established by society to maximize the potential effectiveness of its children and youth-and the counselor, as a part of the school must accept this responsibility. Fourth, logic dictates that more information about the family can be obtained from first-hand observation of the family, rather than reports by the children. Fifth, efficient and proficient referrals of individuals and families by school counselors

> to community agencies maximize the assistance available and enhance the professionalism of school counselors. Finally, increased responsibilities of the school counselor necessitate that all counseling strategies be the most effective possible.

In the "learning systems", counselors should also more actively pursue their consulting roles with school administrators and classroom teachers in broad areas of student needs and concerns, such as course offerings, work-study programs, positive school and classroom environment, meaningful activities, and student representation in school affairs. In the broadening of their professional educational consultation responsibility.

> Counselors should also work closely together with curricular specialists to assist one another when curricular or guidance and counseling objectives are hindered or subverted by school structure and organization. Further, counselors and curricular specialists should develop strategies and tactics in concern to overcome obstacles and rigidities in school structure and organization impeding legitimate outcomes for students. In so doing, counselors and curricular specialists realize that structural and organizational improvements in schools may frequently bring about desired student behaviors just as validly as curricular or guidance measures.

In community systems school counsellors must frequently anticipate a role as career consultants. In this capacity the counselor will plan for the integration of school and community career development resources to ensure their efficient and effective utilization. This suggests that counselors assume a major role in the school's career education program. To this end, school counselors will need to consider the following recommendations.

a. Involve business, labour, community representative, and parents in the development of career education programs as teachers and resource people.

b. Introduce occupational coping skills seminars to assist students in the transition from school to work, e.g., job seeking, interviewing, resume preparation, and self-analysis leading to self-improvement.

c. Sponsor or teach career exploratory courses throughout the school year as a part of the total guidance program.

The effective school counselor in the last decades of the twentieth century must also be able to assess social and psychological characteristics and relate these to educational developments and individual adjustments: be able to identify and recognize the influences of cultures and subcultures on their members: and be prepared to functions as a human resources developer and agent of change in the educational-community setting. Podemski and Childers recommend that

To establish more response by school, school counselors, as a result of their professional training, experiences and organizational placement in schools, are in a position to harness forces that can stimulate the change process and thereby make school systems better learning environments. At a time when counselors and other educators feel greater pressure for accountability than ever before, the counselor is in a unique organizational position to serve as an institutional change agent. In the change agent role, the counselor is concerned with organizational development as well as the shaping and reformulation of the school's curriculum, program, and the organization itself to meet more effectively the needs of students, parents, and the community.

As the counseling and guidance specialist on the guidance team, the school counsellor *must* also function as the guidance team leader. The development of the school guidance program, while involving other educational professionals, must, by virtue of the special knowledge and skills required, be directed by a trained, professional, and certified school counselor. Counselors often have difficulty distinguishing themselves from other helping professionals because their specialized skills and knowledge are not unique to counseling. As Pate notes

> Our knowledge and skills are shared by psychologists, educators, social workers, and other helping professionals. While we cannot claim that counseling has a unique knowledge base, counselor's interpretation of their knowledge and skills into service is an important aspect of our claim to professional status and suggests a place for counselors in a psychological society.

Pate goes on to suggest that

a. Counselors must continue to emphasize the developmental nature of counseling. Our unique contributions are the assistance we give counselees to realize their potential better and our interventions to remove institutional barriers to that realization.

b. Counselors should continue to recognize education as important to their profession, just as they so recognize the field of psychology. Much of what counselors do for counselees is education or re-education. We teach counselees to use their resources and to develop new resources.

c. Certainly counselors can take pride in the profession's historical ties with vocational counseling. Although we should not be content to equate counseling with career counseling, we should remind our pupils that we have a long record of commitment to career counseling.

**Other pupil personnel workers**

Most comprehensive programs of pupil personnel services in schools will include other professionals whose training and anticipated role may share some similarities to that of the school counselor. These include school psychologist, psychometrists, psychiatrists, and social workers, as well as the personnel whose training is more distinctive, such as the school nurse, physician, dentist, and dental hygienist. Each of these professional specialists also has unique contributions to make to the achievement of the school's objectives. However, if each specialist is to make a meaningful contribution, she or he must have some recognition of the roles and specialities of other pupil personnel workers, as well as a recognition of the expectancies normally assigned to him or her. We now briefly examine the special competencies of the more popular of these other pupil personnel workers.

*School psychologist*: The school psychologist is an important and integral member of the pupil personnel team. In most school settings, the traditional responsibility of the school psychologist is to diagnose and study individual children, who are usually experiencing problems in their educational or personal development. In this role, the school psychologist evaluates various aspects of a child's experiences and behavior that are relevant to an understanding of the child's school difficulties and achievements. For this role the school psychologist is trained in the use of psychological tests and also is prepared to engage in individual or group therapy with disturbed children. The psychologist may also aid teacher and parents in understanding the implications of child's behavior. Although the school psychologist has often been thought of primarily as a problem diagnostician, there has been an increased effort in recent years to consider other options. For example, Granowsky and Davis suggested that the school psychologist has an option for three different roles; (1) the diagnostic approach. (2) the community-centered approach, and (3) the administration approach. Based on a rapidly changing society, the authors suggest that psychologists examine their role definitions and select the one that is most appropriate for their particular school. The traditional diagnostic role employs (1) diagnostic testing and reporting; (2) designing educational strategies for pupils and teachers; and (3) evaluating these strategies. Such an approach involves behavioral approaches and classroom intervention and service.

A second role model would be that of the community-based school psychologist. Such a person would operate from a mental health center, be administratively independent of the schools, and act as a consultant to the school staff. Granowsky and Davis state that this model allows (1) the school psychologist to place his or her allegiance with the child rather than the school; (2) direct and more intense contact with the parents; (3) expanded resources utilizing the total mental health center staff; and (4) dual therapy emphasizing educational remediation plus individual growth. The psychologist would, in addition, provide the school with traditional services.

The third role model views the school psychologist as a part of the central administration. The psychologist (1) facilitates the group process and interchange among the professional staff; (2) identifies high priority problems; and (3) organizes an effective team of psychological specialists. The author believe that the school psychologist in this role would be proactive rather than reactive. Based on his or her skill in diagnosis, the school psychologist can assist the school counselor and other pupil personnel workers in gaining a better understanding of individual students and their problems.

The school psychologist can also serve as a resource person for case studies and as a source for referral for certain categories of disturbed pupils.

*The school psychometrist:* The school psychometrist is a pupil personnel worker whose training, background, and job functions are in many instances so similar to the school psychologist that little besides their job titles distinguishes them. However, the school psychometrist is often more limited in training and, as a result, is also more restricted in the kinds of activities in which she or he engages in the school. The major emphasis in the training of psychometrists and on their job performances is usually in the area of psychological measurement. In some school settings, the major contribution of the psychometrist to the school pupil personnel and guidance program may be in the organization and administration of the school's standardized testing program.

*The School social worker*: The role and function of the school social worker, like those of the school counselor, have evolved and broadened from its beginnings in the early 1900s, and have been influenced in heir development by compulsory education laws, new knowledge about individual differences among children, and a recognition of the impact of education and the school on school-aged youth. Today, the school social worker works to eliminate the social-emotional influences that handicap the students's formal education. To this end, the social worker actively workers with the family, school, and community, and seek the involvement and cooperation of parents in facilitating the development of their children. This may involve interpreting to the family their child's behaviour as the school views it and, in turn, receiving information regarding the child's behavior at home. The end goals is to have the parents participate positively in the school-child-parent relationship. The school social worker also functions in a liaison role between the school and community, and is particularly interested in eliminating the community causes of school problems rather than treating the results. In working with the family, school, and community, the social worker seeks to identify and eliminate the base cause of problems. Primary services of the social worker include case studies, group work, and consultation. In the school setting, the social worker is a valuable "Team" member who can make a significant contribution to the in-depth understanding of an individual student's problems through case studies and who also provides significant linkages between the school, home, and community.

*School medical personnel*: Most school systems employ medical personnel on at least a part-time basis. These personnel consist typically of the school physician, school dentist, school nurse, school dental hygienist, and school psychiatrist. These personnel can contribute to achieving a better understanding of the pupils' physical or clinical problems. The school counselor can, in turn, give to these personnel a better understanding of the causative factors of the students' physical and mental well-being. Medical personnel can also contribute to increased counselor understanding of pupil adjustment needs through in-service case studies and consultation.

The potential interrelationships between school health services and school guidance services was noted in the publication *Suggested School Health Policies*, prepared by the National Committee on School Health Policies of the National Education Association and the American Medical Association in 1966. This publication suggested four important aspects of the school health service: health appraisal, health counseling and interpretation, emergency care for injury and sudden illness, and communicable disease-prevention and control. Among the techniques suggested were; continuous observation, particularly by teachers, screening tests; psychological and social evaluation; and health records. The publication also suggested the importance of interpreting pupil health needs to parents, pupils, and teachers. It was also recommended that health personnel be aware of the influence of the teacher and other educators on the aware of the influences of the teacher and other educators on the emotional and social environment of the pupil. Thus, these commonly expressed concerns of both school counselors and school medical personnel indicate their natural allegiance in the development of cooperative programs for the development and adjustment of the individual.

*Other pupil personnel assignments:* In addition to the previously described professionals who, by nature of their training and certification, are specially prepared for their contribution to pupil adjustment and development, others, by virtue of their assignment, are also often members of the pupil personnel team. These individuals most frequently have the titles of attendance worker, dean, director of student activities, and placement director.

*Attendance Worker*: The attendance worker is probably the oldest "traditional" pupil personnel worker. Although most schools no longer label this individual "truant officer', the basic responsibilities of this individual is still in pupil accounting. The emphasis in pupil accounting, however, has gradually changed from threats and punishment to encouragement and remediation. In this role, the attendance officer and the counselor can each provide valuable information and consultation to each other. As an example, it is particularly important that the attendance officer and counselor coordinate important that the attendance officer and counselor coordinate their efforts in seeking solutions to the perennial dropout problem, identifying its causes, consulting with parents of dropouts, and encouraging the reentry of dropouts into school.

*Student Deans*: Whereas student deans have been more traditionally associated with college student personnel services, some high school and junior colleges often employ pupil personnel workers designated as deans of students, deans of boys and girls, or deans of men and women in addition to school counselors. The function of these individuals has often appeared to be one of administering student facilities, activities, and regulations. As a result, they are frequently viewed more as administrators than personnel workers. Students deans have also been frequently cast in the role of the disciplinary agents for the school. In this role, their potential contribution to the school guidance program is discounted by many who contend that guidance and discipline are poor "mix". A number of programs utilize the title of "dean" for their counselors, and traditional "deans" in other programs are trained counselors.

*Student Activities Director:* The director of student activities, as the title implies, is primarily responsible for the administering of the student activity programs within the school. In this capacity she or he may regulate and coordinate student group activities, identify and plan for needed activities, and assess or evaluate the individual activities and the activity program in general. Through cooperation with the school counselor, students may be assisted in participating in activities that will promote their growth and adjustment, serve their interests, and develop their special abilities. At the same time, coordination of guidance activities with other student and school activities can be facilitated.

*Placement directors*: Placement directors are most likely to be found in large secondary schools and institutions of higher education, where their role is primarily on part-time and/or full-time career placement. In addition, at the secondary school level, placement personnel will also be frequently concerned with the placement of students in post high school educational institutions. The increased emphasis of career guidance in the 1970s resulted in a corresponding emphasis on, and an increase in the number of, placement specialists in high schools. Cooperation with the school counselor and school psychologist will enable those responsible for pupil placement more effectively to *coordinate* pupil in terest, abilities, and experiences with placement opportunities and needs. A few schools also have college counselors or placement specialists whose major function is to facilitate the placement of interested and qualified students in a college of their choice.

**The school administration**

As indicated earlier in this chapter, the guidance team for schools consists not only of the professional counseling staff and other trained pupil personnel workers but also the school administrator. The school administrator, who may be a superintended of schools, junior college president, or building principal, is justified in expecting the staff of the school counseling and guidance program to contribute to the achievement of the institutions' objectives. The administrator must also recognize that this contribution will be severely handicapped if she or he fails to realize his or her important responsibilities in the success of this program.

The school administrator represents the educational leadership both in the community and in the specific educational institution as well. In this capacity, it is the administrator's responsibility to give open and recognized support for the school counselling and guidance program. The administrator should also provide advice and direction on budget expectations, physical facilities, ancillary professional and service personnel, and policy guidelines. The school administrator is also responsible for indicating to the school counseling and guidance activities which she or he views as mandatory or desirable in facilitating he goal attainment of the total educational program. In most setting, the administrator will have the primary responsibility for communicating program characteristics, achievements, and needs to school boards and other within the educational system and to the tax-supporting public.

**The classroom teacher**

With the exception of the home, pupils spend a far greater portion of their crucial developmental years in school than in any other type of institution. During these years, pupils obviously spend a far greater portion of their in-school time with the class-room teacher than with any other professional educational personnel. The teacher-pupil relationship is the central, or key, activity in the educational endeavor. It is therefore obvious that other activities in the educational setting which are concerned with the pupils development, adjustment, and total growth must, of necessity, involve those who work closest with them and, as might be anticipated, usually know them best. This means that the classroom teacher is an indispensable member of the guidance team.

The classroom teacher at every educational level has the opportunity to fulfill his or her important role in the school guidance program through functioning in the following ways.

*As a Listener-Adviser*: Mary had been increasingly distracted from her schoolwork and in a rather absent-minded manner had been inattentive in class for more than a week. This was unlike the vivacious, energetic, and capable student Miss Jones decided that at the first opportunity she would examine Mary's record and consult with her school counselor prior to initiation any discussions with Mary. Miss Jones is an example of a guidance oriented teacher who is alert to the needs of her students and aware of the valuable assistance that the school counselor may be able to provide in helping her met these needs. Miss Jones and her fellow teachers at every educational level have countless opportunities to advise, consult, or just act as receptive adult listeners to students and their problems, concerns, decisions, achievements, and failures. This, then, is a primary role and function of the classroom teacher. This role of a listener-adviser does not suggest that the classroom teacher is a counselor in the professional sense (for counseling is a complex, special skill which requires specialized training), but does recognize that she or he is in the front line of the school counseling program.

*As a Referral Agent:* If, in our previous situation, it became apparent that Mary's difficulties were too complex for Miss Jones to handle, a guidance-minded teacher like Miss Jones very likely would discuss with Mary the possibility and advantages of talking with Mr. Haseley, In this capacity, Miss Jones would illustrate the important function of the classroom teacher serving in a referral role in the school guidance program. It is obviously impossible for the school counselor in is or her limited contacts with the total student population to be personally aware of all or even a small portion of students who may be in need of counseling assistance. Therefore, the alert classroom teacher in his or her role as a referral agent can ensure that students with significant problems will not go unnoticed and uncounseled.

*As a Human Relationship Facilitator*: When Johnny entered Miss Jone's class this morning, another pupil in the class spoke a ceery hello to which Johny replied, "Shut your damn mouth" Johny ten proceeded to shove his way ;rudely through a group of girls who were standing near his desk. Coming to his desk, Johny noticed some books of another student on his seat. He kicked them on to the floor saying" They aren't mine! What the hell are they doing here? The classroom provides an interesting have come to recognize the importance of the classroom setting for the development of human relationship skills in the individual student. The classroom teacher then, as the normally recognized leader of the classroom group, as another important role-i.e., that of a human relationship facilitator and developer. This means, first of all, that the teacher reflects and demonstrates good human relationship before and with her or his students. It also means that the classroom teacher plans and directs group interactions which promise positive human relationship experiences for each individual participant. Further, many students will need individual tutoring in developing and mastering these skills, just as in any other type of learning. In the case just cited for example, the ever-alert Miss Jones might plan a strategy for improving his relationships with his fellow students. Even though the teacher is the focus of human relationship development activities in the school, the school counselor should be viewed and used as the human relationship consultant in the educational setting.

*As a Career Educator*: Another important role and function of the classroom teacher, which is emphasized by the national career education movement, is the planned contribution in every subject matter class for ;the pupil's overall career and related educational development. In this role the teacher has the opportunity to provide a data base from which pupils will make their eventual career decisions and to understand the relationships between education and career planning. Indeed, at every educational level, the teacher has the opportunity to provide for career-oriented experiences that are appropriate to the levels of readiness of their students. The classroom teacher must also provide the student with opportunity to examine and develop various care oriented skills and examine roles that may have career applications for him or her in the future. The school's program of career guidance must be centered in the classroom and integrated into the ongoing and total educational program of the institution. Since the total development of the individual is vital, the career aspects of this development cannot be separated from the whole. For the classroom teacher's important role as a career and educational developer, the school counselor can again function as an expert consultant. The counselor can also assist the classroom teacher in securing appropriate educational and occupational development materials and can take responsibility for planning special activities that are related to the ongoing classroom experiences of the student.

Whereas the preceding paragraphs have described at the over all role and function of the classroom teacher as a guidance -minded teacher of guidance team, the classroom of the guidance-minded teacher offers the most natural, consistent, and effective setting from providing pupils with developmental guidance. We, therefore, encourage teachers to seek preparation for their important role on the school guidance team.

**Paraprofessionals**

In recent years education has witnessed and increase in the utilization of individuals who are not by training or experience classified as professional educators. These individuals, who have been labelled most commonly as paraprofessionals or educational aides, have served in a variety of capacities, such as providing clerical assistance to classroom teachers, supervisory assistance to study groups, tutorial assistance to younger and often "Slow" learners, and various service activities, i.e., cafeteria and transportation. Although the coming of the paraprofessional has not been without attending controversies, the economic and facilitative advantages appear to be slowly winning over the opposition that still exists to their employment. The utilization and related controversies of the employment of paraprofessionals in school guidance and counseling programs has closely paralleled that of other areas of education. However a study by Guidance Committee of the North Central Association of Colleges and Secondary Schools seems to indicate both acceptance and an increased utilization of paraprofessionals in school guidance programs. In view of the increased acceptance of the paraprofessional in the school guidance program, four major principal relevant to the role and function of paraprofessionals are examined in the paragraphs that follow.

a. Paraprofessionals are employed only ;when their utilization enables the professionals in the program to function more effectively. Most practicing counselors do not have to review the proliferation of articles in the professional journals to know that they are spending a disproportionate amount of their professional ;time and effort on clerical and other repetitive tasks which do not require their professional skills. The employment of paraprofessionals to relieve school counsellors of such routine chores, is a popular and appropriate paraprofessional role. However, when the paraprofessional is viewed as an alternate to the employment of additions professional personnel with the duties, the guidance program suffers both in image and function, as well as in potential service. This suggests that paraprofessionals should only be employed in those activities which are commensurate with their training and experience.

b. Where employed, paraprofessionals should be provided with opportunities for both training and advancement. If the paraprofessional is an asset to school guidance and counseling programs, his or her contributions to; the program can be further enhanced by a planned training program that seeks to provide the paraprofessional; with additional appropriate knowledge and skills and to prepare him or her for increased program responsibility. The latter would also suggest the existence of career ladders that would enable the professional to anticipate and work toward advancement in school system. In some inward advancement in the school system. In some instances, it may be possible for the paraprofessional to complete a counselor training program and thus move from the role of paraprofessional to professional.

Many community colleges around at the country have developed human services training programs which focus on the preparation of paraprofessionals for work in psychological, social; welfare, and educational agencies and institutions. A few community colleges have also initiated programs that are tailored to a given paraprofessional speciality. Zimpfer notes that a community college program will typically lead to an associate degree, which provides a sense of status and achievement to the student. The opportunities for job advancement are greater for this person than for the lesser-trained paraprofessional. Similarly, the opportunity for transfer into four-year and ultimately even into graduate training, if the student has the aptitude and the desire, is also afforded. Horizontal mobility is also an advantage of a community college program. Because of its breadth, the knowledge and skills acquired by the paraprofessional are often generalizable acquired by the paraprofessional are often generalizable to a variety of settings.

c. Individuals who are selected to work as paraprofessionals in school guidance programs should be carefully screened prior the their employment. As previously stated, school guidance program personnel should demonstrate positive human relationship techniques and understandings. This "modelling" cannot be limited to just the professional staff. Such nonprofessionals as the receptionist, student helpers, secretaries, and paraprofessionals will also be in contact with students and others served by the school guidance program. They, too, are important in the creation of models and perceptions by which others make judgments.

d. Paraprofessionals should function within the ethical guidelines of the professionals they are assisting. Those paraprofessionals who are associated with the school guidance program should be informed of, and expected to function within, those ethical guidelines prescribed for their professional colleagues. This initially means that they must be informed of their guidelines and the resultant expectancies, and that adequate supervision must be provided to ensure their conformity to the guidelines. The objectives of the school guidance program could be thwarted if, for example, paraprofessionals inadvertently broke rules of confidentiality or good human relationship practices.

## The Professional helping team for community agencies

### *Mental health centers*

The Community Mental Health Centers Act of 1963 and its subsequent amendments stimulated a nationwide development of community-based agencies that provided services for the prevention and treatment of mental health disorders. The act originally provided for five essential services: inpatient care, outpatient care emergency services, partial hospitalization, and counsultion and education. Later, additional services, prepare and aftercare services, training, research, and evaluation. These services are available in mental health centers to all individuals who reside in the geographical area designated as the center's responsibility. The inability of individuals to pay for these services need not prevent them from being utilized. No minimum period of residence in the service area is required for treatment. Self-referral or referrals by the family of clients is the most popular approach to the services of community mental health centers. Next in popularity are referrals from family physicians, the legal system, schools, and other community agencies. The professional team for community mental health centers may include psychiatrists, psychologists, social workers, and other mental health personnel, including counselors and psychiatric nurses. In addition to the professional team, administrators and support personnel and even volunteer workers also work in many centers. The responsibilities of the professional staff is dictated by their professional training and background.

**Other Social Service Agencies**

*Small Community-Based Social Service Agencies*: During the past fifteen years, thousands of small, nonprofit, community-based social service agencies have been established. Community-based social-service agencies are those whose scope of operation is focused on the immediate community or on specific needs within a caused on the immediate community or on specific needs within a community and whose principal function is to meet a specific social or human-service need. These grass roots organizations are usually effective, because they are able to take risks, adjust to societal changes, and provide opportunities for people willing to engage in one-to-one relationships with clients.

The staffs of these agencies usually consist of a director, an assistant director or project coordinator, a secretary (usually part-time), and a volunteer support system. Volunteers perform highly specialized functions that require experience and skills as will as odd jobs that require no formal training. The services provided by these small community-based agencies may emphasize or include referral assistance; educational activities such as consumer skills, remedial education, and training for the handicapped; job placement and job training related to placement; and advocacy and outreach functions. The small social service agencies provide assistance to a wide range of individuals; elderly people who have limited financial resources, teenagers "on the run". Veterans involved with drug abuse, family members coping with divorce, recently widowed individuals struggling to deal with their loss, and countless others.

The "team" for these small agencies may consist of only one or two full-time professionals, frequently psychologists or sociologists, "backed up" by a variety of volunteers, and, in some settings, by part-time employees as well.

*Service Agencies for the Aging*: The" graying of America" has led to increased interest in and services for the aged. The largest network of agencies to serve out aging population are those agencies that were established under the 1973 amendments to the Older Americans Act. Approximately 600 agencies nationwide are operative under this act. Each agency is responsible for determining the needs of the elderly in its area and planning a strategy to meet these needs. Roles and activities for which counselors may be particularly well qualified are providing retirement counseling, assisting in adjustments to the deaths of spouses, and providing a vocational and recreational guidance.

Aging agency "teams" are typically headed by the agency program administrator whose staff may include social workers, psychologists, counselors, nurses and nurses aides, and nonprofessional assistants, who are often volunteers.

*Rehabilitation Counseling*: Rehabilitation counselors work with disabled clients to assist them kin overcoming defects in their skills. In these efforts the counselor is seeking to bring physically, mentally, or emotionally disabled adults, this includes entry into an appropriate career. The rehabilitation counselor's role is a complex one and may include providing fro a broad range of psychological and career-oriented services, coordinated with other community agencies and consultation with families and employers or types of clients such as the deaf, blind, the mentally ill, or the physically handicapped. The majority of rehabilitation counselors work for government agencies oar nonprofit organizations. In these settings, they often work in close cooperation with physicians and/or psychiatrists. With the implementation of Public Law 94-142, which provides for the integration of handicapped students be increasingly employed by school systems or utilized as resource personnel to consult with school counselors in dealing with the particular problems that handicapped individuals face in the school setting.

# 6 Educational Guidance

Educational guidance aims to maximise learning in students. The emphasis is on providing assistance to them to achieve the best of their ability in all the prescribed courses of study. Teachers in technical institutions develops instructional plans, implement them and evaluate the effectiveness of their instruction for the main purpose of enabling their students to acquire the knowledge and skill prescribed in the courses of study. Students often encounter difficulties in understanding what is taught in the classrooms, laboratories and workshops. They will be found wanting in achieving the explicitly spelt out instructional objectives a, failures in examinations and tests, poor standards or assignments, unsatisfactory involvement in the academic work by students are some of the often noticed problems. These result in improper utilisation of institutional facilities and resources, unsatisfactory benefits of the efforts of instruction and frustration to students. Efforts must be made to ensure that problems of the above types are solved to the maximum extent.

**Objectives**

The following are the objectives of Educational Guidance:

- To monitor the academic progress of students studying in the institution
- To acquaint the students with the prescribed curriculum

- To identify the academically gifted, backward, creative and other category of special learners
- To cater to the educational needs of special learners
- To assist students in getting information about further education
- To diagnose the learning difficulties of students and help them overcome the same
- To assist the students to maximise their scholastic achievement
- To help students to review and reflect on their performance on the course, and where appropriate to identify ways of seeking changes in work habits or behaviour.
- To help students face the consequence of acceptance of their role and to respond to the demands legitimately made on them.

**Principles**

The strategies that teachers adopt to plan and implement educational guidance must be appropriate to the problems for which guidance is needed. The following are some of the principles on which educational guidance must be based

- Educational guidance must be objective oriented
- Every student is capable of achieving the best of his ability
- Individual differences in academic achievement of students must be recognised
- Educational guidance strategy must be student oriented
- The strategies must take into consideration the resources and facilities available to the students

- Educational guidance is not for a few students only; it needs to be provided for all.

**Classification**

A class in which all students have more or less the same abilities for coping with instruction is ideal for teaching-learning. Teachers may employ the same instructional strategy for an entire group of students whose entry behaviour characteristics, learning ability, interest motivation, attitude to learning are the same. In such situations they do not encounter much difficulty in guiding students for optimal learning. In reality, classes are never homogeneous and teachers have the challenging task of coping with a variety of students' characteristics. Students in any class can be ordinarily classified into three categories viz., the average, below average and above average on the basis of their academic performance. The below average students are those whose performance is below the average performance of the class.

Those whose performance is above the average of the class are categorised as above average. In this category, we may notice creative and gifted students as well. There are other types of students called slow learners, who have the ability to perform satisfactorily but are only slow in doing so. Their slowness may be attributed to a combination of a variety of causes. There may be some students, whose performance in comparison to that of the class may be satisfactory. Yet, their own performance may not be commensurate with their ability.

**Identification**

Problems in learning are most common in all categories of students. An above average student is likely to have as much of learning difficulties as a below average one. By providing educational guidance, efforts must be made to ensure that students maintain their level of academic performance. In all other cases, the efforts should be towards enabling the students to overcome their educational difficulties. In doing so it is important to identify those students who have problems and find solutions to their actual problems.

Identification of students is possible by continuous and careful observation of the 'academic behaviour' by teachers. The aspects of behaviour that may be observed include the interaction of students with the teacher during instruction, the types of questions put by them, interest shown for involvement in the teaching-learning activity, keenness exhibited for learning, alertness in grasping whatever is taught in the class, performance in tests and assignments, perusal of assignments and other assigned work. Teachers can easily observe their students in the classes. However, care, must be exercised in drawing conclusions based only on observation. For, a student who may be shy to answer questions or ask questions should not be identified as a weak student. It is important to spot out those students who require educational guidance not only on the basis of observation, but also on the basis of discussion with other faculty.

The following are some of the tests that may be used for the purpose.

### *Achievement Tests*

Achievement tests are used to find out what has been learned i.e. what habit and skills have been developed in students as a result of instruction. They are valuable as a means of determining to what extent the student has attained a certain degree of progress towards a desirable goal, whether he is ready to undertake the next step and how his attainment compares with that of other members of his group. These tests, based on the prescribed syllabus enable the teacher to find out the strengths and weaknesses of the student. It is possible to find out the improvement on achievement. Diagnosis which forms one of the basic steps in providing guidance is possible through achievement testing. Achievement tests serve a variety of purposes for use in educational guidance programmes. These are useful to survey students in order to find out those with educational problems, diagnose the actual difficulties and for prognosis. The survey type of achievement tests comprise items that include the content covered in a subject area in order to find to what extent students meet the accepted norms and standards of academic performance. Diagnostic tests serve the purpose of finding out the actual weaknesses of students. Prognostic tests are to determine a student's readiness for learning.

#### *Aptitude Tests*

Aptitude of a person is latent trait accounting for the probability of his Success in a field related to the traits on giving necessary training. Aptitude is a combination, of inborn capacities and developed abilities, skills etc., that makes the person what he is at any give time and predicts what he may become. Aptitude tests are expected to measure the potential for specific abilities and skills such as music, graphic arts, medicine, law, engineering, teaching etc. They tell us how well the individual is equipped to excel in a specific skill. They may indicate future superior achievement in the particular skill or ability tested. Whether or not a potentiality attains realisation depends upon various factors-willingness of individuals to engage in appropriate study and practice, quality of the training provided, public interest in and demand for the exercise of his special ability.

### *Intelligence Tests*

These are used to determine an individuals' learning capacity. The results of intelligence tests may be used to arginase learners into relatively homogeneous teaching learning groups. It is important to note that a fairly high degree of mental alertness is required in pursuing various courses of study. Learners who have low intelligence level experience learning difficulties, if they choose certain types of courses. It has also been found that success in certain vocational areas is dependent upon a high degree of intellectual ability.

### *Interest inventories*

It is well known that success in any course of study or vocation depends to a considerable extent upon the interest the individual takes in it. Interests are closely related to aptitude. In certain cases interests are intrinsic. In most cases, interests to be created externally (e.g. giving prizes, high salary, perks, praise etc.) This provides a constant incentive to continue until the goal is reached. It must be noted that worthwhile activities are better supported by intrinsic interest, because the pleasure continues even if the goal is not reached.

Finding out the interest (or appraisal) is difficult. However the methods used are to ask the individual about their interests, to analyse the various activities in which the individual is involved, and measuring interest using interest inventories. The first two methods have obvious limitations. While in the first case, the individual's oral explanation cannot be relied upon very much in the latter case, individual may be involved in work because of necessity. It would be difficult to find out whether the activity involved is freely chosen or chosen out of compulsion. A number of standardised interest inventories are available to teachers for use in different situations for a variety of purposes.

**Ethics in collecting guidance information**

Information or data about an individual's personality achievement, interest, aptitude etc., are very vital for any guidance activity. The data obtained must be valid and reliable which, therefore, implies that the tools used for collecting such data must have high validity and reliability. Certain points are to be kept in mind about the information collected.

Whenever a test has to be administered to an individual it should be done in a relaxed and friendly atmosphere. The test should never be thrust upon him. He should never be allowed to take it when he is under stress or strain. Readiness to take the test' is an important aspect. Test scores should not be disclosed to any other person than the student himself without the explicit knowledge and permission of the client. Strict confidentiality has to be maintained whenever the data needs to be used for research purposes, special care is to be taken to see that the identity of the student is not at all revealed. Any information provided by him either as responses to test items or interviews should be treated confidentially.

Whenever a test is to be used for vocational and educational Purposes (selection to a job, admission to a course) the test sample should not be disclosed... It might be useful, if information is provided about the nature of the test, the traits it measures, how to prepare for it, etc. It is highly unethical to provide practice or coaching for the test. A test should never be administered to a client because the teacher 'knows' it. He must administer a test in which he is trained and competent to administer. Professionally it is prestigious for a counsellor to know the limits of his competence and to clearly state these limits to his clients.

***Tests and their uses***

| *Area* | *Name of the test* | *What type* | *For whom* |
|---|---|---|---|
| Intelligence | Standard Prog ressive materices | Contains 60 patterns | Adolescent students |
| | Group Test of General Mental Ability | Verbal test containing 100 questions in 9 areas | For 15 years and above (including adults) |
| | Bhatia's Perfor mance Test of Intelligence | Performance test with 6 subjects | 11½ to 16½ years old students |
| Aptitude | Mechanical Apti tude Test by Atmananda Sharma | Verbal test containing five categories | Adolescent students |
| | A Comprehensive Scale of Enter-preneurship | Verbal test containing of 6 sub scales | Adolescent students |
| Interest | Singhs interest Record | Verbal test consisting of 168 items | Students in the age range 13-18 |
| | Thurstone's In terest Schedule | Verbal test | Adolescent students and out of school adults |
| Achievement Motivation | Achievement Motivation Test by Prayag Mehta | TAT Type | Adolescent students |
| | Level of Aspirations Test by Shah and Bhargava | Verbal test | -do- |
| Study Habits | Patel"s Study Habits inventory | Verbal test consisting of 45 items in 10 areas | Adolescent students |

**Guidance folder and master register**

Guidance is a time consuming process and several sessions will be required to provide adequate guidance. Each session may result in some new facts emerging which can provide some nearer insights into the problems of the individual concerned. The information so emerging should be very carefully recorded. Further sessions may have to be based on this information. Obtaining information alone is riot important but storing the same is equally important. The work involved in recording and filing is tedious and uninteresting yet, most important. The record should be cumulative and, in addition to up-to-date identifying data, should include important items concerning a student from the time he enters the institution until he leaves it. Such information about a student car, be stored in a guidance folder. This is designed to cover a period of years. Suggested items for guidance folder are: Identifying data, home background, economic condition, health record, academic record, out-of-class activities, character and personality traits, special or peculiar incidents (details), special interests and achievement, educational plans, vocational plans, experiences, details or outcome of each guidance/ counselling session.

Particular care must be taken in maintaining the folder. The entries must be made as accurately as possible. Where tests are administered, the date, time and conditions under which the tests were administered has to be correctly recorded. When interpretation of information is recorded, it has to be done under specific headings. Guidance folders should be made available to the concerned teacher as well, since the learner's aims, interest, potentialities, degree of accomplishment, application to work represent valuable data to teachers in evaluating classroom work and in guiding learning. There is one exception to this general procedure, confidential information about an individual that is of value~ only to the counsellor should either be removed from the folder before the latter is made available for general use or be kept in a separate file.

The information collected about students must be properly recorded. It is suggested that a master register may be developed for the purpose. The register may contain information about the different aspects of all students such as their place of education, medium of instruction at the school, study habits, level of motivation, performance in tests and assignments. Great care must be exercised in filling up the record sheet for each student. This sort of a register can be used for maintaining information about all students of a class.

**Strategies for educational guidance**

Teachers must build educational guidance as an integral Part of their everyday instruction. Every teacher consciously or otherwise, deliberately or not deliberately attempts to provide, guidance to their students in learning. Sometimes it may be given in a formal way and at. Other times in an informal manner. The guidance may range from suggesting/advising students to be systematic in their studies, to planning and implementing individualised instructional strategies.

***Strategies***

Educational Guidance Strategies to be used by teachers depend upon the nature of the problems, and the extent of their effect and the purposes of providing for such guidance. These strategies should be situation oriented and student-oriented. The strategies employed must help in enabling students to achieve to the best of their abilities in scholastic areas. Guidance and counselling strategies can be classified into two categories viz., group approach and individual approach.

*Group approach*

Every student must have the freedom (and be helped) to choose the courses of study considering his educational ability, interest, future needs etc. The purposes of this type of guidance are

- to encourage students to utilise their abilities in specific areas
- to assist students in understanding and appreciating the instructional obligations which they are required to complete. This may include information regarding the assignments, tests, project work they are required to complete as part of the course work
- to provide information to students regarding further education programmes
- to give general orientation to students regarding the facilities and resources available such as library, laboratories, workshops, scholarships etc.
- to provide opportunities for group thinking in regard to common problems and experience

*Procedures*

Group guidance approach for educational purposes must be organised for disseminating educational information of a general nature to students. Care must be exercised in organising group guidance; Group guidance may be in the form of group discussion and talks to enable students to plan their educational activities. This is possible by giving them information about the courses of study, curriculum requirements, scheme of evaluation etc., by teachers.

It is advisable to organise group guidance sessions for students who have common problems by identifying, students. Poor achievers, students whose level of motivation is low, those whose study skills are not satisfactory may be provided guidance, through a group approach. However each of these categories of students must be given appropriate guidance.

The following steps may be followed in organising group guidance programme

- Determine the areas in which guidance is to be organised.
- Identify the themes to relate to the areas spelt out
- Plan appropriate and alternate approaches to involve students in the programme
- Evaluate the strategies and implement the same
- Spread out the group guidance programme during the year
- Involve all the faculty in the programme
- Evaluate the effectiveness of the programme
- Organise follow up

Besides the general group guidance programmes, teachers may have to design and implement group guidance in their own class for the purpose of general improvement in academic performance. Such guidance must form an integral part of instruction. In these programmes, teachers may have to often focus on the progress of the students, common problems faced by them and suggestions for overcoming them, common mistakes, committed in tests and assignments and suggestions for improving their performance. For effective organisation of group guidance it may be necessary to have a team of faculty for planning, implementing and evaluating these programmes. The team members have to be properly identified with one of them, preferably a Head of Department as the coordinator of the programme. The task of the team would be to

- identify the areas and scope of guidance for students
- plan a schedule of guidance programmes spread throughout the year
- decide the strategy such as lecture, conference, seminar, etc. appropriate for the spelt out objectives
- conduct the guidance programmes as per the schedule drawn
- evaluate the effectiveness of the programmes organised to get feedback for purposes of improvement
- plan and monitor the follow up.

**Induction programme**

Several problems of students in the area of learning may be attributed to a lack of knowledge of what the institution can offer and how it can do so. This calls for a knowledge of the facilities and resources available in the institution. These facilities may be laboratories, workshops, library, recreation, cocurricular, hostel etc. Each of these are meant for specific purposes, work under a set of rules and regulations, have certain expectations from students. It is important to have an understanding of the rules and regulations of the academic administration of the institution. Certain areas under which such information is required are attendance requirements, scholarship and stipend awards (conditions for award, criteria and mode) academic and extra curricular activities, guidance services rendered by the institution.

It is not that such information is not provided by institutions. Some institutions give these as part of their prospectus which is supplied with the application form for admission. Most often students do not go through the rules. It is taken as a routine information. Even when the same is read, it is read rather casually. Thus, the purpose of giving the information in the prospectus gets defeated. The practice that should be followed in institutions is to hand over a copy of the rules and regulations and get the students committed to these. It is only then that they try to adhere to the same.

Institutional induction is an activity which is in tended to 'introduce' the institution in its totality to the students. It is during such an activity that students come to know of the objectives of the institution, its development, traditions, resources, faculty etc. This activity enables the students to know the environment in which they are required to work/study. It lays the foundation for their continuous interactions at the institution. It enables them to accept the institution as a place where their needs would be met, their aspirations and goals fulfilled. Students will be able to see themselves in the context of the institutional environment.

The aim of induction programme are to

- Assist students to understand the tradition, and distinctions achieved by the institution.
- Enable students to know the facilities and resources available in the institution.
- Help students to become familiar with the various programmes, and activities, both curricular and cocurricular organised in, the institution.
- Help students to understand the administrative set up and rules and regulations of the institution.'

**Organisation of induction programme**

The objectives spelt in the above paragraph can be realised if induction programmes are efficiently organised. The main intention of such programmes should be a mutual understanding involving the students, staff and the administration of the institution. The beginning of the academic programme would be the most ideal period for the organisation of induction programmes. In fact, all the academic activities planned by the institute should follow this programme. Care should be taken to cover all aspects of the life of students during their stay in the institution. It is also advantageous to introduce all members of the faculty and office of the institution to the students during these programmes. A visit to the different departments and laboratories including the library will be very useful. A well drawn time table for the induction programme goes a long way in its effective implementation. It is useful to involve all members of the faculty in the organisation of such a programme.

**Hints for planning induction**

The following hints may be borne in mind in planning and conducting an induction program

- Spell out clearly the objectives of the programme
- Identify the appropriate content/theme for each objective spelt out
- Determine the suitable strategy for achieving the objectives spelt out. The strategies may be lecture, discussion, visits to the, library, laboratories, video presentation etc.
- Identify the faculty for each sub activity
- The programme must provide opportunity for students to meet all the faculty of the institution
- Prepare a time table for induction programme and make the same available to all students before the start of the programme. A sample of induction programme is enclosed.

**Guidance for special learners**

Special learners are those who stand out as a distinct set from other students in a class and therefore require special attention. Educationally they deviate from the average students in their academic achievement. These learners require special attention by teachers. They do not profit much from learning in average group situations.

Special learners in institutions may be classified as

- Gifted
- Creative
- Slow learners
- Learners with difficulty for learning.

Gifted students are those who show consistently remarkable performance in educational endeavours. They possess a superior intellectual potential and functional ability to achieve academically in the top 15 to 20 per cent of the students in the institution, and/or talent of a high order. Creative students are those who exhibit creativity. Creativity is the process of sensing gaps missing elements; forming ideas or hypothesies and testing, the same. It is the ability to change one's approach to a problem, to cope with ideas that are both relevant and unusual; to go beyond the immediate situation to redefine the problem.

Slow learners are those students who require more time for learning than the normal/average students in a class. Hence, they show marked educational deficiency. They learn at a slower rate than others. In order to provide guidance to the above category of learners it is important to identify them. For these learners, individual guidance will have to be arranged. Identification of the special learners will have to be carried out systematically. It may be based on teachers' observation, academic records and performance in mental ability traits.

**Guidance for learners with learning difficulties**

The following strategy is suggested for providing guidance to students who have learning difficulties. The following are the steps for Guidance for overcoming learning difficulties.

- Observe the interaction style of the student in the class, their assignment and other records
- Administer specially designed diagnostic test
- Identify the students for guidance purposes
- Analyse the causes for learning difficulties
- Plan alternate approaches for overcoming the difficulties
- Implement the approaches
- Evaluate the approaches

**Guidance for under-achievers**

Under-achievers are those students who do not achieve to the extend they can. The following steps may be followed in guiding such learners.

- Administer an achievement test to the entire c
- Identify the students who need guidance
- Assist them in resetting goals
- Plan and implement appropriate strategies for guidance.

**Guidance for gifted learners**

The following steps are to be followed in guiding gifted students.

Identify the gifted students on the basis of

- Observation of student characteristics, their interaction style, quality of assignments and projects completed

- administering tests of intelligence

Select the most appropriate approach for catering to the gifted. The approaches are

- segregation of the gifted and arranging classes exclusively for them
- acceleration through which students may be allowed to complete the prescribed course of study in a shorter period than normally taken by the rest of the students of the class.

Enrichment programme through prescribing enriched/additional/depth content and suggesting additional books and journals for study by students

- project and assignments

— evaluate each approach in relation to the constraints and restraints for implementing the approach

— Implement the selected approach.

# 7 Vocational Guidance

One of the most satisfying experiences in human life is that of creativity; the creative process is essentially that of a search, and this search is inseparable from a process of work as we have so far defined it. It is impossible to avoid the suggestions of sexuality in this: to create is to give birth, whether physically in woman after her labour; or to new ideas after a period of creative disturbance; or to an object after mental and physical labour on it. It is also associated with the release of aggression and even with the concept of war: to gain victory after struggle and after sustaining intermittent defeats in which the individual may have felt not only his self-confidence, but his personal integrity, threatened. A successful outcome to a creative struggle is in fact the outward projection of part of the individual's life force; in the newly born child, the completed boat, the beautiful garden, the individual sees a material assurance of his own identity, and even at times a kind of immortality. Just as work is central to the creative process, so this in turn provides the context within which work takes on its deepest significance. Boris Pasternak once wrote: 'the fabulous is never anything but the commonplace by the hand of genius,' and genius itself has been described as an capacity for taking pains. Even at its highest level, the transformation of the mundane involves a process of work. These thoughts give us the possibility of refining our definition of work: in its most significant from, work is the sustaining of tensions, or risks, and intermittent failures, inseparable from the process of forming new ideas and giving them material reality. Seen in this light, then, work should always be involved in some way with the realisation of at least some part of the worker's dream: it should express, however imperfectly, some aspect of that world of phantasy that once gladdened his childhood's play; it should symbolise, in part of from time to time, the deeper values of the worker's life. The idea, sometimes heard, that a child passes in adolescence from a phantasy view of the world of work, to a reality view of it, seems to miss the fact that human development is normally a continuous, unfolding pattern in which the past can never be dismissed or neglected. When an individual is required to work for long periods of time, usually out of economic or social necessity, at tasks which afford him to opportunity whatever for any expression of his personality, both the concept of work and the individual are thereby degraded, and the destructive effects are no doubt proportional to the length of time over which such a situation continues.

Much, but not all, of peoples' work takes place in the context of earning a living, or following a career, and for ease of discussion let us call this 'employment'. A man's employment of course includes its social setting: the people he meets in the course of his employment, and the social recognition which his employment affords, both of which are important influences on his attitude towards it.

Employment roles usually require a fairly massive commitment of work, and this is a good point at which to examine some of the broad possible consequences of this. The most satisfying employment is one which presents challenges that we can meet by a deep and creative personal involvement. This is usually seen as a good thing, and we are apt to forget some negative sides of it. Success here, as elsewhere in behaviour patterns generally, is likely to be followed by a deeper involvement. This can usually be justified, if the need arises, but the requirements of 'earning a living' or 'following a career.' If progressive improvements is accompanied by increasing success, the employment may begin to draw in too much available energy, and insidiously to attenuate the private life, which may become correspondingly shallow. Too much work now take place in one setting only-the employment role-and is not sufficiently distributed over the broad spectrum of life. Whether this is seen as a good or a bad thing depends greatly on the social values that are accorded to private life, the family, religion, and so on. These may well vary from one society to another. A friend of mine, who once worked in Africa, found that the attendance of his labour force was rather erratic. One day, when very few men had turned up, he went out and found one of them, a huge negro, lying on the side of the road with his hands behind his head. "Why are you not at work?' He asked. And got the reply: 'for a long time now we have had very hot, wet, unpleasant weather: this is the first good day, and any sensible man will lie on his back in the sun.'

One specific aspect of a deepening involvement with a employment role is, however, worth a special mention: a tendency to use it to compensate for failures in private life, and to evade the need for more effort there. Work-especially creative work-can take the mind off other things, and release the tension generated by frustration elsewhere. Persistent evasions of this sort may well amount to a rejection of life itself, impossible to justify except by rare creative genius in the employment role.

At the other extreme are employments which are potentially creative, but in which the individual has failed in the sense that the cannot involve his deeper life with the work, whose functions he discharges in a mechanical way; and employments which are basically sterile, such as many forms of factory labour. In the first of these we may find the imitator-the individual who conforms over-closely to the style of clothing, the turns of speech, the ways of thought, the patterns of activity appropriate to his employment role, as a compensation for a deeper failure there. 'Action', wrote Canard, 'is consolatory. It is the enemy of thought and the friend of flattering illusions.' This over-identification with the trivia of the employment stereotype may extend into many distant and apparently irrelevant areas of life, so that in extreme cases we may say with the scathing words of Volatire about an acquaintance: 'he was born a man, and died a grocer.'

If, on the other hand, the work offered by the employment role is both demanding and boring, the concept of work itself may be rejected wholesale, leading to the use of non-creative, non-demanding leisure activities upgraded out of all proportion to their value. Harold Entwhistle has emphasised the high likelihood that boring employment leads to the dull and unimaginative use of leisure: a man whose brain has been dulled by eight hours of monotonous toil can hardly be expected to burst into creative leisure activity: in short his ability to work has been damaged. It is perhaps significant that throughout history we see examples of those sections of the population engaged in the dullest, most routine work, putting a high value on non-demanding 'viewing' activities, from the circuses of ancient Rome to the football stadiums of today.

**Implications for vocational guidance**

How far does vocational guidance, as practised in our schools, stand up to examination from this viewpoint? Nearly everywhere, in the practice of vocational guidance, it is assumed that work means employment, and this is particularly clear in the description of the various offices and activities in this field, such as 'careers officers,' 'careers teachers,' 'careers convention,' 'careers literature,' and 'work experience'. The over-emphasis on this association of work with employment reflects a general failure to think deeply enough about the meaning of work; and implies an acceptance of the popular idea that work and leisure are different things. Perhaps this is partly the price of an empirical approach to guidance generally, with its unwillingness to explore concepts at the abstract level. The idea of a clear distinction between work and leisure certainly needs to be broken down, perhaps by more attention in training programmes and conferences in counselling, to the definition and discussion of goals and assumptions. If it is not, there may be some future danger of the spread of courses and programmes of 'education for leisure', carrying further the artificial distinction already present in the terms we looked at earlier. Where pupils can be encouraged to relate ideas which they find personally exciting, to those which they associate with work, the basis of a new approach exists, meaning, in effect, the marriage of vocational guidance to counselling.

However, the question of how far children should be encouraged to express their creative energies through employment *alone* is very complex, and illustrates the impossibility separating vocational guidance from the need an overall philosophy of life. At one extreme is a certain view of employment as a 'job' void of anything worthwhile; a daily interruption of life; at the other extreme is the obsessively employment-dedicated man to whom nothing but a career matters. Proponents of the first viewpoint sometimes take a 'realistic' or 'tough-minded' approach to the formation of employment-attitudes, and hence to vocational guidance. They argue that at the present time, and in the foreseeable future, many forms of industry will require large reserves of manpower for the dullest and most routine jobs. For such people education should concentrate on the creative use of leisure; and in any case, not encourage a false view of the world of work, among those most likely to fall into routine employments. Such unimaginative attitudes ignore the onrush of automation, the increasing geographical mobility of urbanised societies, and the whole background pattern of change, which we look at in the next two chapters, and which, however materialist its methods and aims, is swiftly changing the approach of many young people towards their vocational futures. The question which adolescents increasingly ask, in Britain and elsewhere, is not how to find a good job, or to make a career, but whether to bother about such things. I have little sympathy with those who dismiss such young people as being simply lazy: their problems seem to me to arise out of a deeply sincere questioning of the worth of modern urban civilization. The spread of cynicism about accepted values, the rejection of the 'establishment,' of authority, seem to me to go wider than the characteristic and temporary rebellion in adolescent development against the older generations; and as we shall see later, even in communist countries there is some evidence of a similar trend, masked by lip-service to stereotype ideals. The drift of this wind through our societies further illustrates the change of separating vocational guidance from counselling.

Why in fact has the development of guidance in semi-specialised from in British schools, been so closely identified in the past with careers work? Why have these simple and essential ideas about the relationship between work, leisure, and personal development not been sufficiently considered to lead guidance away from a narrow pre-occupation with employment, to a wider view of life goals? The answers probably lie in the tendency in British society, which we have looked at, to concentrate on processes rather than on concepts; on immediate problems rather than on long term goals. Thus the earliest government intervention, represented by the Employment Acts of 1909 and 1910, set up juvenile departments in some Employment Exchange to help place boys and girls in jobs, and to allow Local Education Authorities to do this also. To be fair, the wording of the Acts and official memoranda at this time indicate a recognition of the need for guidance on a wider basis; but in practice the provision become one of job-placement, predominantly for the children of the poor. The excessive concentration on job-placement has remained as part of the official attitude towards vocational guidance, in spite of various attempts at improvement, and in spite of being drawn much more closely into the frame work of L.E.A supervision since 1948. Why did the concept not evolve faster? There are several possibilities. One is the fact that guidance structures existed outside and independently of the schools: the contact between Youth Employment Officers and school staff was too fleeting for serious discussion of deeper issues in guidance. The fact that an organised structure existed outside the schools; and school heads, often tending to think of the successful pupil as one who made the ascent into a university or teacher-training college, may, as we have suggested earlier, have thought of an early leaver looking for a job, as an educational failure. Also, for many years, the use of psychological tests was almost totally unknown among teachers, so that no independent pointer to the relationships between personal, educational, and vocational needs of children was available.

But the main reason why for so long the idea of guidance lay at the level of job-placement in Britain is almost certainly to be found in the social stratification of education. The acceptance of new ideas in guidance and the rise in the numbers of careers teachers, and the emergence of the counsellor as a new figure in schools, co-incide closely with the rise of comprehensive secondary schools. We have already emphasised the tendency of grammar and public school heads to judge success in terms of educational attainment. This limited the development of the concept in those areas. In the secondary modern schools which emerged after the 1944 Education Act, a large number were situated in industrial slum areas, where the prospects, career or otherwise, were too grim to think about. Here there was little or no incentive to start thinking along sophisticated lines about guidance. But the comprehensive schools which emerged a few years later were in a different position: they offered a diversity of educational opportunity at the secondary level unknown in the other kinds of school, and extended deep into adolescence the problems of educational, vocational, and personal choice. In such circumstance, especially in the larger schools, sense of uncertainty, even of being lost, can easily emerge, and for the young pupil soon grow to formidable proportions among so many new faces, both of pupils and staff, most of them stranger. In such a situation, the development of an effective guidance system, able to make contact with such pupils is completely necessary if the main aims of the school are to achieved: one can go further and say that it is the presence of such a system, and its efficient functioning, that largely holds the balance between a comprehensive school approaching its ideals; and an 'education processing factory' of the kind described by opponents of the comprehensive school principle.

In fact, the sort os situation we have suggested here has involved fairly specific problems, and their solution has here has involved fairly specific problems, and their solution has encouraged the emergence of *techniques*. The newcomer has to be introduced to the school; at its simplest this means making certain that the pupil understands what opportunities are open to him, and how to use the main lines of communication. Pupil records have to be developed beyond the simple report-card stage, in order to record as much as possible of the kind of information which, in a smaller community, would be casually picked up by teachers in getting to know their pupils. The advantages of using psychological tests as a short-cut to objective information have begun to be recognised, and teachers involved in guidance work in comprehensive schools frequently seek courses at which they can build up their knowledge and experience with such instruments, and so improve the quality of the record system. There has been considerable attention to the formation of guidance teams, and to the use of team work techniques to help overcome the communication problems in big establishments, and to deal with the wide diversity of problems encountered. These developments, as Moore emphasised in his study of five such systems, have taken place response to immediate problems, and, judging by the growing importance attached to them, seem to have met with a good deal of success. As we have already seen, movements of this kind tend to call for role-differentiation, and specialists of the kind or another tend to appear in the teamwork, leading naturally to the question of appointing a personal counsellor, or counsellors, for the pupils. The tradition of guidance, as employment-centered vocational guidance, was of course inadequate to meet this need, and hence the importation wholesale of the American theories and practices of counselling.

But the solutions worked out from the 1950's onwards, and increasingly throughout the 1960's, were in terms of how to develop and integrate *new areas* of guidance to meet the peculiar problems of big schools, and not generally in terms of deeping thinking about the existing concepts-especially, of vocational guidance. The goals were seen in terms of the solution of immediate problems. Thus it happens that we can only say that vocational guidance in Britain has evolved during the last two decades, if by 'evolution' we mean the expansion and refinement of provision, not of concepts. This means that a difficulty is sometimes found in how to relate the specialist in vocational guidance to the specialist in personal counselling, in the organisation of school guidance to the specialist in personal counselling, in the organisation of school guidance teams. In some such patterns the careers teacher actualy appears as an additional specialist *outside* the main guidance team, itself organised around a system of pwesonal counselling. Again, in some schools, counselling is dominated by a concept of vocational guidance crudely centred on helping the adolescent to make a happy 'first-job' choice, which of course means that the emphasis is on the early leavers rather than over the whole school population. Again, some at least of the confusion that exists about the difference between 'counselling' and 'guidance' stems from the fact that there has been a continuous development of provision in this semi-specialist area, but as a result of the failure of the concept to evolve, there is now a spilt between a concept which began in Britain, and a similar one, which evolved in a totally differednt fashion in North America, and was then imported into Britain in its matured form, as counselling, in the 1960's. As an example of this difficulty, an authorative article in *New Era* in 1968 stated that vocational guidance was essentially *informative,* and should be handled by careers teachers, whereas personal guidance was essentially *problem centred,* and constituted the main role of the counsellor in secondary schools. Likewise, vocational guidance is still seen by the Youth Employment Service in terms of employment-guidance. In this however the Service is not to blame, being hamstrung by its terms of reference.

Underlying all these questions about the relationship of vocational guidance to couselling are of course big questions about the relationship between the individual and his society, and about social duties. While we shall touch on some of these issues in the second part of this book, we can immediately turn to look at the institutional framework within which the various guidance functions take place, and by which they are also partly shaped and limited.

# 8 Psychological Tests

A psychological test has been defined in varied ways. According to Anastasi, "A psychological test is essentially an objective and standardised measure of a sample of behaviour."' Freeman writes, "A psychological test is a standardised instrument designed to measure objectively one or more aspects of a total personality by means of samples of verbal or non-verbal responses, or by means of other behaviours."' Most of the psychologists are of the opinion that a psychological test is a pattern of stimuli selected and organised to elicit responses which will reveal certain psychological characteristics in the person who makes them. A psychological test is like a test in any other science, in so far as observations are made upon a *small but carefully chosen sample of an individual's behaviour.* In this respect, the psychologist proceeds in much the same way as the chemist who tests supply of water by using one or more *samples* of it. For example, the psychologist who wishes to test the extent of a students' mechanical comprehension, examines his performance with a *representative* set of problems. The *diagnostic* or predictive value of a psychological test depends upon the degree to which it serves as an *indicator* of a relatively broad and significant area of behaviour. It is not essential that the test items in a psychological test resemble closely the behaviour the test is to predict. The degree of 'similarity between the test sample and the behaviour to be predicted may vary widely. Sometimes, the test may coincide completely with a part of the behaviour to be predicted just as in a language test, the test items relating to language proficiency are given. In vocational aptitude tests, there is a *moderate resemblance* between the operations performed on the job and those incorporated in the test. But in projective personality tests such as Rorschach Inkblot tests there is absolutely no resemblance between the test situation and the behaviour to be tested. Here an attempt is made to predict from the subjects' association to ink-blots how will he react to other people, to emotionally-toned stimuli and to other complex everyday situations. It is obvious that a psychological test is an effort to quantitatively measure the various aspects of behaviour of the individual in such a way that we can make generalised statements about his total performance and behaviour.

A good psychological test, must possess the following essential characteristics:

1. *Validity*—By test validity we mean the degree to which the test actually measures what it claims to measure. It tells us what can be inferred from test scores. It is specific to the purpose and the situation for which a test is to be used. For example, a test of general intelligence which has been validated for rural population cannot be used for the purpose of knowing the general intelligence of urban population and vice versa. That means before using a test, we must know the test is "valid for what". It is only after determining the specific *criteria used* in validating the test and the *group on* ~,which the validity was conducted, that the counsellor can decide whether the test is suitable for the purpose for which ]he uses it or not.

There is another aspect of validity *data-the magnitude*

*or the size of correlation-A* high correlation would signify that the testee who scores high on a test will be an outstanding success in the specific course or career and the one with low scores will be an abject failure.

2. *Reliability*-Reliability means the accuracy with which Me test measures a particular trait. It shows "How good is this test"? Test reliability is the consistency of scores obtained by the same person when retested with the identical test or with an equivalent form of the test. Reliable tests, whatever they measure, yield comparable scores upon repeated administration.

The reliability coefficients for a test give the evidence of the consistency of performance of students either in one period (split-half method) or two testing periods separated by a short interval (test-retest method). For making accurate predictions ;about testees, relatively high reliabilities are required.

3. *Objectivity*—Administration, scoring and interpretation of scores should all be independent of the subjective judgement of the individual examiner. The scores should be identical regardless of who happens to be the examiner.

4. *Standardisation*—A good test is a standardised measure to be able to compare different individuals. It is necessary that materials employed in the test, time limit, oral instructions to be given to the testees, preliminary demonstrations, ways of handling queries from testees and every other detail of the testing situation, the surroundings, etc. are standardised and guidance regarding all these be made available in the test manual.

5. *Norms*—Norms are scores which are typical or characteristic of pupils of a given age or grade. Only that test is a good measure which provides appropriate and accurate norms, whether they be in

the form of age, grade, percentile rank, standard score, etc. These norms should be meaningful with regard to the purpose for which the test is intended and to the groups of persons with whom it is to be used. Test norms should be derived from a sample of individuals who are comparable to the individual for whom the counsellor wishes to use the test. It is also important that norms provided in the test should indicate not only the average performance but also the relative frequency of varying degrees of deviation above and below the average. This is necessary to enable us to evaluate the different degrees of superiority and inferiority. Local norms of the test selected for use should also be available so that a common base line is there which could be referred when interpreting an individual's score.

6. *Simplicity*—Simplicity and ease of administration, scoring and interpretation is another important characteristic of a good test. This is particularly important when expert personnel or an adequate budget are not available.

7. *Economy*—It should be possible to administer the test in a short time; this will help gain the cooperation of the subject. It will also save time of all those involved in test administration.

8. *Interesting*—Last but not the least important, the test should be interesting. Test that is interesting and enjoyable will encourage the subject, and it will be possible to elicit useful information.

Man is a complex creature. He possesses different traits as intelligence, aptitudes, interests in different measures. His achievement also differs. There is also a great difference in the personality makeup of people. With the background of all these differences, the individual has to make various choices-choice of courses and careers, choice of playmates and roommates, choice of life-partners and lifestyles. To help him in all these and make his journey smooth and satisfying, there is an utmost need of some objective measurement. The psychological tests of varied types are being used by teachers and counsellors, doctors and psychiatrists, administrators and psychological experts, civilian and army personnel in almost all countries of the world. The psychological tests in different areas are supposed to meet the following pertinent needs:

(i) To help students at choice and critical points when they have to make a decision: The psychological tests can provide the client or student with information about himself in relation to a series of choices where the decision would be his own. Objective quantitative data plus subjective observations and assessments' are needed to enable him to make a correct choice. For instance, the single factor that Deepak's parents will be highly disappointed if he does not go in for architecture can decide Deepak's choice in favour of architecture. But if the quantitative data is also available signifying the capacity of Deepak to go in for architecture, the situation becomes simpler and satisfactory decisions can be arrived at. Similarly, psychological tests can help a student to decide whether he should continue his studies or take up business. The scores on the interest inventories will enable him to find out whether his interests are those of a scholar or those of a businessman.

(ii) To enable the counsellor to have a broad-gauged look and uncover as many promising opportunities as possible for the counsellee: It is important for the counsellor to survey as many of the skills and abilities of his counsellee as he can in order to arrive at a judgement as to which areas of endeavour are likely to be most promising. It is not enough, in a guidance setting, to know that Gurpreet has medical aptitude; if he has also the makings of an electronics engineer, Gurpreet and the counsellor need to know that too. It is important that a number of psychological tests are used to uncover as many promising opportunities as possible to enable the counsellee make an ultimate choice based on broad knowledge and enable him to get his goals towards the highest and most personally rewarding vocation

(iii) *To enhance the client's ability to make his own decisions:* Students in schools, colleges and universities have to make decisions regarding the selection of courses, co-curricular and extracurricular activities. Studies have revealed some disconcerting insights into the ways such choices are made. Often such random factors as having friends in the field, the chance encounter with a particular course, the influence of a teacher who made the subject mean enough to merit further effort, were the determining ones. When such an important choice is made by chance or because it is a relatively safe or easy choice, or because the personality of the teacher is charismatic, the impetus towards. A discipline can be essentially external rather than a commitment to the field as a body of knowledge. Thus many decisions, in fact, may be made on the basis of chance, situational factors, e.g. a charismatic teacher or family pressure or perhaps an unexamined personal factor. Psychological tests can be used ~to provide some additional basis for a decision.

iv) *To help teachers to adapt teaching to the need of students:* *If* the teacher could get objective assessment *of* the interests and capacities *of* students with the help of psychological tests, he can adapt his teaching to the needs of students. He can also differentiate between the slow learners and underachievers and help them according to their needs.

(v). *To help the counsellors.* Modern schools provide individual counselling for pupils with respect to their educational and vocational plans. Many schools also provide for maladjusted pupils some sort of clinical service. The psychological testing is an integral and accepted part of the fact-finding phase of counselling. Wise counsellors use the meaningful and relevant data obtained from the tests as a partial basis for their client-centered interviewing and clinical judgments.

(vi) *To help in satisfying an administrative need for selecting the most promising pupils from among the applicants:* True, in a democratic society, pupils should be allowed as much latitude of choice as possible.

Also the selection of curricula should be based on sound counselling. But at times it does become important to select the most promising pupils for the good of individuals and society. Psychological tests help here..

(vii) *To help establish homogeneous groups:* Psychological tests can be used to help establish homogeneous groups within elementary and secondary school systems and college setups. Placement in a class appropriate to the student's potential can accelerate development and improve self-concept.

(viii) *To provide information for selection, classification and distribution of clients, to serve primarily the interests of the particular administrative system:* Psychological tests can be used by admission committees in schools and colleges to sort applicants into groups. They can also be used by school and college systems to classify and distribute students across various curricula. Thus if we could know that ability level A, interest pattern B, achievement level D and extracurricular activities grading S, relate to successful performance in a professional college, then the college can use the test results in future too to assign students to either the medical or non-medical group. Tests can be used, and properly so, to serve allocation functions and to provide data for distributive decisions about clients and students.

(ix) *To help in the selection of students for special schools for the award of merit-cum-means scholarships for residential schools in the country:* There are so many schools in the country, to which children from weaker sections of society can be admitted provided they possess the superior native ability. This can be found with the help of psychological and standardised achievement tests.

(x) *To help in the selection of students for admission to special institutions:* There are a number of special institutions as National Defence Academy, Khadak-wasla; Indian Military Academy, Debra Dun; Air Force Academy, Hyderabad; Naval Academy, Cochin; Armed Forces Medical College, Poona, etc. in the country. There are also a number of professional colleges and institutes. Psychological and standardised achievement tests are used for admission to these institutions.

(xi) *To help in the distribution of personnel in various branches of services:* For example, the defence would like to recruit persons for the Armed Forces who are above average in intelligence and emotional stability; are of higher level in mechanical and clerical aptitudes; are fit and fine physically. Such persons as are perfect from every angle are not easy to get. Thus the military psychologist is faced with the problem to find out the special qualities required for certain special jobs in army. Psychological tests are needed for measuring the special qualities or traits so that on the basis of the scores, the recruits could be sent for special jobs. The persons who obtain high scores on mechanical aptitude tests can be put on mechanical duties; the persons who can work with speed and accuracy, may be put in charge of the office work. That way the psychological tests can be of immense use for putting the right man at the right place.

(xii) *To help in the psychological diagnosis of students:* In any school/college system there are a number of students who have moderate to severe emotional problems which impair their learning ability. The estimates of emotional problems usually run from 8 to 15 per cent of almost any sufficiently large population or group; a school/college setting is no exception. There is an obvious need for differential diagnosis of these difficulties as a first step toward appropriate treatment or remediation. A careful analysis of the student's intra-psychic balance, or a critical appraisal of the student in relation to the environmental pressure, is necessary. An identification of learning disabilities rooted in the student's past experiences is essential. The pupil can be given a carefully selected battery of personality tests specifically designed to tap information about the personality makeup, with increasing emphasis on psychological dynamics. For example, the examiner may use an individual test of intelligence, a sentence completion test, a Thematic Apperception Test and the Rorschach Ink Blot Test. The results of such testing are essential for decisions to be made about the pupil. The assumption is that the pupil's difficulty or emotional adjustment is of such an order that he cannot make his own decisions. In the long run, that would be harmful and selfdefeating. If the test results confirm this assumption of extensive emotional difficulty and inordinate interference with normal behaviour, then the results may also indicate the appropriate course of action to follow for the client. For example, the test information could provide a basis for referral to a "special class'~ or "special form of treatment."

(xiii)*To help the teachers in dealing with the scholastic and behavioural problems:* For making decisions regarding pupils facing problems of conduct or scholarship, comprehensive measures of achievement, together with standard measures of achievement and the school record itself, provide factual bases of great importance for reaching a sound clinical decision regarding any boy or girl.

(xiv)*To identify abnormal patterns in the personality of the client:* For those students whose personality encumbrances place them outside the range of normal behaviour, whose past experiences so significantly influence their present perception that they literally cannot accurately perceive reality-for these students, accurate appraisal of their personality is essential. The power and initiative for decisions cannot be left to the student in the grip of emotional disturbance. Psychological diagnosis forms the basic data and the necessary information about the client which the psychological expert may use as a legitimate and systematic basis for selecting the appropriate course of action for the client.

(xv)*To help in the treatment of psychiatric problems:* When a patient comes to a mental hospital or clinic, it is essential to find out what type of person he is and how will he respond to the treatment. Psychological tests can be helpful in taking this crucial decision. Carefully constructed and wisely administered psychological tests can provide good measures of the abilities, aptitudes, interests, attitudes and personality traits. They can help in diagnosis and prediction, selection and classification and are of immense use in many situations and jobs.

**Counsellor's use of psychological tests**

The counsellors may use the tests to:

(i) *secure accurate and reliable information about each student's abilities, interest, and adjustment problems in order to give him proper guidance and counselling.* Proper understanding of each pupil's strengths and weaknesses can help the counsellor to help the counselling in a more meaningful way;

(ii) *make use of test results for further performance.* Tests can provide an improved basis for prediction regarding the likelihood of success in those activities in which prospective performance can be measured;

(iii) help students arrive at decisions basic to planning their educational and vocational future;

(iv) *diagnose students' problems.* Problems like social adjustment, growth and development or academic deficiencies may be identified and plans for their amelioration may be mutually determined; and

(v) *help them evaluate the outcomes of guidance and counselling, and plan further remedial programme.*

**Limitations of psychological tests**

Psychological tests are good instruments for measuring different human traits. However, they have some limitations:

(i) *Human behaviour is often subtle and the psychological forces, motivating or influencing persons in a test situation, may be elusive and difficult of evaluation.*

(ii) *The quantitative data* of *psychological testing are not as definite, precise and uniform as are the data of physical measurements.* Also, the interpretation of test findings is quite difficult.

(iii) *It is not possible to determine the inherent difficulty* of *an item* in *a psychological test in terms* of *the constant units, as it is possible to find the length or weight* of *any object.*

No direct measurements and comparisons are possible in psychological tests

iv) Classification by ability measures *proves detrimental.* The classification labels of bright, average and particularly that of inferior based on psychological tests go through the school and college career of individuals. In the words of Murphy, "The struggling and starvation go on in schools, hospitals, clinics, families, wherever we freeze our expectations of a child in terms of the belief that tests are the truth, the whole truth and final permanent truth about a child's potentialities. Judgements are too often weighted on the negative side."

(v) *Psychological tests reflect cultural background of a race or social class, hence are not valid and reliable instruments for measuring ability and achievement of all students.* No wonder children born and bred in a culturally different environment are penalised because their experiences limit their effectiveness in a test situation.

(vi) *The tests used in our institutions give a partial view of the students' capacity.* Many psychologists are of the opinion that testing fosters limited conception of ability, achievement and personality. They feel that tests are based heavily upon verbal and quantitative skills that do not encompass all types of achievement needed in our society

(vii) Perfectly valid and reliable tests are not available

**Major classifications of psychological tests**

Psychological tests can be classified into eleven major types on the basis of *content, objective, medium, traits* to be measured and the main use for which they are prepared.

*Maximum and Habitual or Typical Performance Tests:* Cronbach suggests two main types of tests-tests which measure the maximum performance of an individual, and tests which measure habitual performance. The former correspond to ability tests, the latter to personality tests. The object of ability test is to discover how well the individual can perform in a certain area, under the most favourable conditions. In personality tests, it is the usual or habitual reaction of the individual that is sought, not what the individual believes is the best solution. "Roma gets tense when he differs with his superiors" describes the reaction of the individual in a specified situation. Paryag Mehta's Test of General Intelligence is an example of maximum performance test and Rorschach's InkBlot Test, and Bernvequter's Personality.

2. *Individual and Group Tests:* For the administration of test, it needs to be known whether the test can be administered to an individual or to a group. For instance Bhatia Battery, and Stanford Binet Test can be administered to individuals, Raven's Progressive Matrices Test of Intelligence and Chatterjee's Interest Preference Record Card can be administered both to individuals and groups. Individual tests enable the examiner to observe the subject's work methods, his social and emotional reactions, etc. These tests also give the examiner a better opportunity to establish rapport, obtain cooperation and maintain the interest of the subject in the test. Any special conditions which may handicap the subject in is performance can also be noted and remedied. Individual tests generally require a highly trained examiner. They are designed primarily as clinical instruments for the intensive study of individual cases.

3. *Paper-Pencil Tests and Performance Tests:* In the Paper-Pencil tests, the subject is provided with a test form or test booklet which contains all these items. Responses are written by the subject on either the test form/test booklet or on a separate answer sheet.

Chatterjee's Interest Preference Record, Raven's Progressive Matrices Test of Intelligence, Differential Aptitude Test Battery are some of the examples of Paper-Pencil tests.

Performance tests require motor or manual response on the examinee's part, generally but not always, involving manipulation of concrete equipment or materials. They involve a minimal use of paper and pencil. Performance tests are also used in another sense, to denote tests which are actually work samples. In this sense, they may include the use of paper and pencil. For example, in a performance test in accounts or shorthand, materials other than paper and pencil may not be required but the test response will be called a Performance Test.

Performance tests are specially useful for

(a) *Deaf* testees as they are generally deficient in linguistic development.

(b) Testees with *speech defects* who cannot give oral replies or are unable to take a Paper-Pencil test.

(c) *Illiterate* testees who cannot take the usual individual or group test that calls for a certain amount of reading and writing.

(d) *Foreign* testees who because of foreign language background may experience special difficulties in taking Paper-Pencil tests.

Performance tests give an estimate of an intelligence of a practical nature as contrasted with verbal intelligence. Thus they can prove useful for guidance purposes. Such tests can also be used with borderline mental defectives. They can alert the examiner to possible problems such as brain damage. Performance tests have some limitations. They have to be administered individually or in small groups. That way, they are time-consuming. No performance test can be totally culture-free.

4. *Language and Non-Language Tests:* In language tests language is used; in Non-Language tests language, neither written nor spoken, in neither the instructions nor the test items is required. Non-Language tests are specially designed for testees who are illiterate, unfamiliar with the native language, deaf testees or others who for some reason are unable to take a language test. Such a test can either be a performance or a Paper-Pencil test. In a Paper-Pencil language test, the test content generally consists of pictures, diagrams and non-linguistic symbols and the subject is required to respond by making relatively simple marks. Instructions are given by gestures, pantomimes and demonstrations involving charts and diagrams.

For most testing purposes, however, it is not necessary to eliminate all language from test administration, since the examinees usually have some knowledge of a common language. Moreover short, simple instructions can usually be translated or given successively in two languages without appreciably, altering the nature or difficulty of the test. But none of the Non-Language tests requires examinees themselves to use either written or spoken language.

5. *Verbal and Non-Verbal Tests:* They can be designated as reading and non-reading tests. In the former reading and writing are required, in the latter neither reading nor writing is required but these tests make extensive use of oral instructions and communication on the part of the examiner. Such tests frequently measure verbal comprehension, such as vocabulary and the understanding of sentences and short paragraphs,

through the use of pictorial material supplemented with oral instructions to accompany each item. Unlike the nonlanguage tests, they are unsuited for foreign language speaking or deaf testees.

6. *Criterion-Referenced and Norm-Referenced tests:* Criterion-Referenced tests describe the performance of the testee in terms of the specific behaviour he can demonstrate (e.g. he can type 60 words per minute without error). It measures the effects of instruction. Norm-Referenced tests describe the performance of the testee in terms of the relative position he holds in some known group (e.g. he can type better than 80 per cent of his classmates). It discriminates between high and low achievers. Teacher made and standardised tests of achievement fall in the category of Norm-Referenced tests. They are designed to rank students in order of achievement, from high to low, so that decisions based on relative achievement could be made with greater confidence. Criterion-Referenced test is deliberately constructed to yield measurements that are directly interpretable in terms of a specified domain of instructional relevant tasks.

Mastery tests are typically Criterion-Referenced and survey tests tend to be Norm-Referenced.

7. *Informal Tests and Standardised Tests:* Informal tests are constructed by classroom teachers, standardised tests are designed by test specialists and administered, scored and interpreted under standard conditions.

8. *Speed and Power Tests:* A speed test is one in which individual differences depend upon speed of performance. The items included in such a test are of uniformly low difficulty level, all of which are well within the ability of the subjects taking the test. The time limit is so short that no one can finish all the items. The individual's score reflects only the speed

with which he works. The test is intended to measure the speed of response. Clerical speed and Accuracy Test in Differential Aptitude Test Battery is an example of speed test ' Similarly, a Card punch operator may be evaluated on the number of cards per hour he can accurately prepare. A camptometer operator might be judged principally on his speed and accuracy with simple computations. Other skills in the general field of clerical or manipulative work may similarly be tested by speed of functioning.

A power test has a time limit long enough to permit everyone to attempt all items. The difficulty of the items is steeply graded and the test includes some items too difficult for anyone to solve, so that no body can get a perfect score. This test is intended to measure *level of performance.* For example, a mathematician is one who can solve complex mathematical problems; a person who can add two-place numbers rapidly and accurately may be a skilled clerk but not necessarily a mathematician. Thus, both speed and power tests are designed to prevent the achievement of perfect scores. To enable each individual to show fully what he is able to accomplish, the tests provide adequate ceiling, either in number of items or in difficulty level. Most of the psychological tests depend upon both speed and power.

9. *Culture-Fair Tests:* These tests are language-free. They also attempt to eliminate skills and feelings that vary from one culture to another. A classic example of such type of test is the Goodenough Draw-a-Person Test, which requires only knowledge of human body.

10. *Tests measuring Traits in Different Areas:* Psychological tests have been constructed for measuring traits i different areas as intelligence, aptitudes, intere attitudes, personality, etc. On this basis the test be classified into three categories (i) Tests of C

Intelligence, (ii) Tests of Special Aptitudes, (iii) Tests for measuring personality.

Most of the types of tests mentioned above are used in the three categories. For example, in Tests of General Intelligence, some are individual tests and others are group tests; some are verbal tests and others are non-verbal tests. This differentiation is also available in special aptitude and personality tests.

11. *Tests for special uses:* Psychological tests can also be classified on the basis of the use to which they are put. Thus we have tests for a comprehensive assessment of mentally retarded; tests for persons with diverse sensory and motor handicaps.

It needs to be emphasised that the different classifications given above have been suggested to help in understanding different types of tests and their purpose. The distinctions are getting blurred as more and more tests and test batteries have been developed. Most of the recent batteries and tests are cutting across these categories. The combinations of verbal and performance tests in the Wechsler scales and their Indian adaptation by P. Ramfinga Swamy and development of Mixed Type Group Test of Intelligence in Bindi (Verbal and Non-verbal) by P.N. Mehrotra are classical examples.

**Use of psychological tests**

The usefulness of psychological tests depends upon their proper use which implies proper selection, careful administration, objective scoring and sensible interpretation.

***Selection of tests***

A great care needs to be exercised in the selection of psychological tests. Only those tests should be chosen which help in the achievement of the objective and are suitable to the level of the testees. The tests chosen should be valid and reliable. They should be standardised on a fairly good sample and should have proper norms. They should also be simple, economical and interesting. The mobility of test equipment and material should not be difficult. The scoring and interpretation of the test should be simple and easy.

*Administration of tests*

Administrators and counsellors expect to use the results of the tests for important purposes often to influence the lifelong careers of the testees. Nothing less than first class administration of a psychological test is fair to the testees. Bingham points out that the accuracy of any measure is quite as much a function of the way the instrument is applied as it is of the instrument itself. The administration of psychological tests requires careful planning and preparation in the following areas:

*(i) Advance preparation*

Advance preparation is one of the most important requirements of good testing procedure. This helps in foreseeing and forestalling emergencies and ensuring uniformity of procedure. Advance preparation for the testing session can be done in a number of ways:

(a) *Test Directions—The* examiner should read the test directions. In order to be fully familiar with the directions, he should read the manual and master the directions before hand

(b) *Test Materials*—Preparation of test materials is another important preliminary step. In individual testing and especially in the administration of performance tests, the material needs to be properly laid out to facilitate subsequent use with a minimum search or fumbling. Materials should be placed on a table near the testing table, so that they are within the reach of the examiner but do not distract the testee.

In group testing, the number of test-booklets and answer-sheets to be used in each group should be counted out and placed in large envelopes. Each envelope should be marked with pertinent information such as room number, teacher, date and time of testing and the number of test-booklets and answer-sheets in the envelope. A few extra copies should be included for emergencies. Packing the tests in envelopes facilitates their return with proper identification to the person in charge of testing After the test is over, the test copies-both used and unused-should again be counted to see that all have been collected.

*Pencils—For all* types of answer-sheets, sharpened pencils with erasers should be provided and the examiner should have an extra supply of pencils on hand to replace those whose points are broken during the testing period.

*Timing Device—In* order to obtain meaningful scores on the tests, it is necessary that the administrators adhere to the standard time limits. Stop watch, wall clock with sweep second hand, wrist watch or pocket Watch with sweep second hand-any one of these should be arranged.

*(c) Rehearsal of procedure:* The procedure needs to be rehearsed with one or more trial subjects. The best method for a teacher who intends to give the test to his pupils is to give the complete test for practice to another teacher or some pupils who will not be included later in the test proper. Such an experience would equip the teacher to administer the test without difficulties.

Rehearsal of procedure should also include the advance briefing of examiners and proctors, so that each is thoroughly familiar with the functions he is to perform. In general, the examiner reads the instructions, takes care of timing, and is in charge of the group in any one of the testing room. The proctors hand out and collect test materials, make certain that subjects are following directions, answer individual questions of subjects within the limitations specified in the manual and prevent cheating. They should observe the pupils from various points in the room and promptly respond to help in case pupils have any difficulty in following the directions.

(d) *Place:* The room in which the tests are to be administered should have good light. The temperature of the room should be comfortable and the room well-ventilated. It should be free from undue noise and distraction. It should have adequate seating facilities and working space for the subjects.

(e) *Time:* Testing should be scheduled at times when students are fresh and alert and when interfering activities are least likely to occur. The morning is suggested if half day sessions are to be used.

Tests should not be given outside of school/college hours or when any distracting activity is taking place. For instance, a class should not be held for testing at an hour when other classes are engaged in unusually interesting activities, such as attending a movie or being dismissed early for a match.

(f) *Testing conditions:* Establishing rapport is one of the necessary parts of the testing procedure. As far as possible, the examiner should make sure that the testee is ready to put in the maximum work.

The specific techniques for establishing rapport will vary with the nature of the test and the type of tests. For example, in testing, problems of the students to be considered include "distractability," "negativism" etc. A friendly, cheerful and relaxed manner on the part of the examiner helps to reassure the testee. Similarly, the shy, timid testee needs more preliminary time to become familiar with his surroundings. So it will be advisable for the examiner not to be too demonstrative at the out set but rather to wait until the testee is ready to make the first contact. The testees can be motivated through an appeal to their competitive spirit and their desire to do well on a test. Some reassurance will have to be given at the outset because no one is expected to finish or get all the items correct. The element of surprise also needs to be eliminated from the test situation, since the unexpected and unknown are likely to produce anxiety. Efforts also need to be made to eliminate the element *of* anxiety. This can be done by making the announcements in an objective, straightforward and matter-off-act manner. It is also important that the testees understand the purpose of the test. This will help in getting their cooperation. Most testees can be made to realise that an incorrect decision can be the result of invalid test scores.

Thus every possible, effort needs to be made for establishing healthy rapport with the subjects to get reliable and valid test scores.

**Testing procedure**

The following procedure needs to be adapted for testing.

(i) *Seating*: The testees should be seated sufficiently far apart to make cheating difficult. Alternate row seating should be considered if the regular seats are very close together. Students should not be seated close to or directly facing one another. There should always be enough room for proctors to pass between the rows. Whatever tables may be used, it needs to be ensured that students have sufficient working space, left-handed students should be seated so that they and their neighbours will be comfortable.

(ii) Pass out answer-sheets to the testees. Instruct them about filling in the identifying data at the top of the answer-sheets and check to see that it has been properly filled in by all.

(iii) Distribute the test booklets.

(iv) Explain that if a pencil is needed, the testee should raise his hand and the proctor will bring him one.

(v) Follow the directions for giving the test. The examiner should have adequate familiarity with the directions. The printed directions should be read word for word in a loud, clear voice. They should never be paraphrased, recited from memory, or modified in any way It is essential that the examiner stays within the meaning of instructions. Changes in the directions would create complications and destroy the comparability and understanding of the test results. Examiners should, in no case, give new examples. If necessary, the given example may be read again.

(vi) Care should be taken to ensure that all the subjects have understood and are following the instructions. After the directions have been read, and during the testing period, some testees are likely to ask questions. It is usually permissible to clarify directions and answer questions concerning mechanics, for example, how to record the answer.

As already stated the examiner should stay within the meanings of the directions given in the manual. If the manual states that the testees should be referred back to the directions, this should be done. In some scholastic aptitude tests, the ability to follow directions is a part of the test and to clarify the directions is to give unfai assistance to the testees. Where it is permissible to clar directions, care must be taken not to change or mo the directions in any way during the explanation.

(vii) Accurate account of the time should be kept. To ensure accurate timing, a written record of the starting and stopping times should be made. This should be in terms of the exact hour, minute and second as follows:

Time limits must be adhered to rigidly. Special care must be taken in timing speed tests as Clerical Speed and Accuracy, Any deviation from the time limits given in the test manual will violate the standard conditions of administration and invalidate the test results. If, for example, the pencil of a testee breaks during the test, and the testee does not have another pencil ready at hand, or the examiner/proctor fails to provide the pencil in time, the test should be marked invalid and not scored.

(viii) During testing, the pupils should be carefully observed and significant events should be recorded. Any unusual behaviour of the testee--tension and anxiety, carelessness-all should be recorded. Similarly, if there are interruptions during the testing a record should be made of the type and length of the interruption and in what manner, if any, it altered the administration of the test.

A record of unusual pupil behaviour and significant events provides very useful information for determining whether test scores are representative of the pupil's best efforts. It is also a check to find out whether, standard conditions have been, maintained during testing. Questionable test scores need rechecking by administering a second form of the test

(ix) After the test is over, the test copies, both used and unused, should again be counted to see that all have been collected. This must be done before the candidates leave the room. It is of the utmost importance that no student or parent or unauthorised teacher be allowed to retain any test copy for study.

Allowing this is considered professionally wrong, and also may invalidate future testing.

**Scoring of tests**

Accuracy is an essential requirement of all types of scoring. Speed and economy are essential in large scale testing programme so that prompt results could be obtained at less cost.

**Scoring individual tests**

The individual tests, whether of the verbal or performance type, are generally scored by the examiner. While administering the test, the examiner goes on recording the testees' responses on a printed record form. Some tests such as Stanford Binet Test, Bhatia Battery, need to be scored during the process of test administration, as the presentation of further items depends upon the testee's performance on prior item. There are some individual tests which could be scored later. As the subjective judgement enters into the evaluation of any response, the results obtained by independent scorers should be checked on a representative sample of record sheets. This check provides a measure of one aspect of the reliability of the test.

***Scoring group test***

Speed and economy are major considerations in group testing. The scoring can be done manually by hand or by machine.

***Hand scoring***

The scoring of psychological tests by hand is a routine clerical task. The procedure consists mainly of comparing the pupils' answers on the test booklet, or separate answer-sheet, With the correct answers listed on a scoring key and counting the number correct. In some cases, such as where a correction formula is used, simple arithmetic skills are also involved. The hand scoring procedure is quite simple but untrained scorers make frequent errors in counting answers, following instructions, using scoring guides and the like.

Such scoring errors need to be guarded against. This can be done by providing supervised practice in scoring the test, getting each paper rescored by a second person.

**Machine scoring**

A number of electrical and electronic scoring machines are available for accurate and quick scoring. International Business Machine (IBM) is quite popular. This machine uses special answer sheets. Answers are recorded on the sheet by blackening the answer space with a special soft pencil. For large scale testing programmes, machine scoring is the most efficient.

**Reporting and recording**

After the psychological tests have been scored, reporting and recording process starts. The test results have to be made available to the teachers, counsellors, psychiatrists, anybody who is mainly concerned. The minimum information to be reported and recorded is (i) the date the test was given (ii), grade in which the test was given, (iii) test title and form used, (iv) total and part scores, expressed in appropriate units, and (v) nature of norm group, where percentile or standard scores are used. If the test has been used with the school/college/university student, it is essential that the information is recorded in the student's cumulative record card so that the comprehensive information is available to the teacher and the counsellor.

**Interpretation of test scores**

An adequate selection, counselling, and remedial programme warrants proper interpretation of test scores so that wrong choices and decisions could be avoided.

For proper interpretation of test scores, it is essential that test, testee and test-situations are properly understood. The measured trait can only be determined with reference to the special conditions under which a test is validated. Any additional information related to reliability, the nature of the group for which norms have been prepared, the background information about the testees, etc. are all required for proper interpretation of tests. A single score can be obtained by testee due to different factors. So, the results derived from these scores can be different. Besides, some special factors as extraordinary conditions for the administration of tests, emotional or physical condition of the testees at the time of test administration, any fresh experience, response sets, or previous experience of the testee with the test etc., should all be taken note of. So, at the time of interpreting the individual test scores, the counsellor needs to remember that the results may be influenced by many factors such as:

i. The physical and emotional condition of the testee at the time of taking the test.

ii. The cultural experience of the testee which may be too limited or different from that demanded by test items.

iii. Errors in or scoring the test.

iv. The validity, reliability and norms of the test.

Adequate time should be provided by the counsellor in his schedule for test interpretation for all testees particularly of those testees who have made low and very high scores. Test results should be interpreted to parents/guardians who wish to know them. However, numerical raw scores should not be given to them, since these are likely to be misunderstood. It is better to use descriptive terms such as 'he belongs to the average group of students', 'he is among the top 20 per cent of students in his class', or 'he should be able to do superior work in a Medical College'. Conferences with teachers should be held periodically for interpreting test results to them with the aim of increasing their understanding of the students they teach.

The testing programme in a school/college/university should be planned to help students understand themselves and to assist them in their educational and vocational planning and understanding their personality. Students should, therefore, be given an opportunity to find out their own strengths and weaknesses as revealed by the tests. Counsellors should be ready to interpret the test results to them. The data as revealed by tests should be considered, in relation to the other information obtained from different sources as anecdotal records, questionnaires, diaries, case studies, interviews etc., as well as from peers and parents, tutors and advisers teachers and administrators.

The following cautions need to be borne in mind for the use of psychological tests:

(i) The sale and distribution of' tests should be limited to the *qualified examiners:* The necessary qualifications will depend upon the type of the test. Thus, for many individual intelligence and personality tests, very long and intensive training is required and for achievement and trade tests, a period of short and special psychological training is required.

(ii) *Test scores should reach only those persons who are capable of interpreting them:* Not only should the scores be interpreted by capable persons, the counselling facility should also be available for those who may become uncomfortable by the knowledge of their scores. For example, a maladjusted student can be upset when he knows his scores on a personality test.

Similarly, a student with high scores on an intelligence test can become careless and uncooperative when he comes to know that he is much better than his classmates.

Whether the scores are correct or not, these harmful effects can be there. Even if the test has been administered and scored properly and has been interpreted in a proper manner, without an opportunity for discussion, the information can harm the individual. The possible harm can be all the more intense when the score itself is wrong. The testee should clearly understand the purpose of administration of the test.

# 9 Counselling for Physically, Emotionally Disabled

In the popular mind, a handicap is physical in nature. The physically handicapped are highly visible and their problems and successes are readily noticed. As a group they comprise the most heterogeneous group of exceptional children. They may have a wide range of medical diagnoses and greatly varying special education and support services needs. Some will not be classifiable as handicapped for special education purposes. Many will be educationally retarded, usually due to lack of experiences or suitable adaptations. They may have problems of personal, social, and emotional adjustment possibly related to the physical impairment, that is, somatopsychic, although the presence and degree will depend on the makeup of the individual pupil. There are also some myths associated with this heterogeneous subpopulation. One is that they possess special educational gifts to compensate for the physical impairment. Obviously, such gifts would be a matter of individual pupil. There are also some myths associated with this heterogeneous subpopulation. One is that they possess special educational gifts to compensate for the physical impairment. Obviously, such gifts would be a matter of individual differences related to aptitude, compensation, and availability of time. Another myth is that the physical impairment is accompanied by a mental limitation. It is easy to generalize the handicap because it is so visual and, at times, limiting in terms of participation in school activities.

**Classifications**

With this subpopulation it is not uncommon to differentiate between a disability and a handicap. The disability is the measurable constant condition and the handicap is a consequence of the disability. This distinction is probably useful for his group in that many do not, or do not want to, qualify for special education programming. As pointed out by Sirvis, want to, qualify to, qualify for special education programming. As pointed out by Sirvis, "it is not the actual physical variation but, rather, the individual's attitude in relation to society's view of physical conditions that determine the extent of the handicap". All classification systems rely heavily on medical diagnosis and degree of functional defect. P.L. 94-142 yields the following classifications and descriptions.

> "Orthopedically impaired" means a severe orthopedic impairment which adversely affects a child's educational performance. The term includes impairments caused by congenital anomaly and impairments from other causes.
>
> "Other health impaired" means limited strength, vitality, or alertness, due to chronic or acute health problems such as a heart condition, tuberculosis, rheumatic fever, nephritis, asthma, sickle cell anemia, hemophilia, epilepsy, lead poisoning, leukemia, or diabetes, which adversely affects a child's educational performance.

A more specific breakdown can be made into the broad categories of neurological, orthopedic, infectious disease, and other health impairments. Thee is always a danger in generalizations made from inclusion in broad categories due to overlap, but the technique is useful as a point of departure for purposes of educational planning.

*Neurological impairments*

Neurological impairments involve the nervous system and generally prove to be more educationally handicapping than other kinds of physical disabilities since the nervous system is the activation of the whole organism. Pupils so impaired present a particular challenge to pupil services staff due to the fact that impairment of learning may compound the physical disability.

1. Cerebral palsy describes a number of neuromuscular disabilities that may range from mild motor incoordination to almost complete helplessness. Prevalence estimates vary according to definition and classification but a reasonable estimate would appear to be three per thousand. In addition to the motor problems there are usually secondary handicaps that impede sensory ad receptive functions. The most prevalent secondary handicaps are speech impairments and mental retardation.

2. Epilepsy is a convulsive disorder that results in some kind of seizure. Brain lesions result in uncontrolled neuron firings in the brain or idiopathic and may be either permanent or temporary, depending on etiology. The seizures are usually described as grand mal, petit mal, and psychomotor. The latter form has been of interest to youth workers because some deviant behaviors, including antisocial behaviour, has been traced to this malady. Epilepsy can be controlled by medication but may have as sequelae some drowsiness, poor concentration and incoordination. Prevalence is about one per hundred.

3. Multiple sclerosis is a disorder of the central nervous system characterized by the hardening of the protective covering on nerve fibers. Symptoms include muscle weakness, unsteady gait, and sensory complications. It is a disease of older adolescents and adults and tends to progressive deterioration. Management of the condition involves interpretation of the condition to the individual, provision of a protective regimen, and appropriate treatment.

**Orthopedic impairments**

Orthopedic handicaps comprises musculoskeletal conditions that effect the limbs, spine, and joints. These conditions may handicap a pupil in terms of mobility or coordination, either gross or fine. Such conditions may be either congenital or acquired. A partial listing follows.

1. *Scoliosis* is a condition involving curvature of the spine which can cause limited movement. It will most likely require casting ad bracing.
2. *Rheumatoid arthritis* involves inflammation of the joints, tendons, and muscles. Frequently, there is severe inflammation of the eyes. It represents one of the few conditions where the incidence for girls is higher than for boys. It is more common in children than is generally recognized.
3. *Muscular dystrophy* is a disease characterized by the weakening of the skeletal muscles. In children the form of the disease is called pseudo-hypertrophic or Deschesne. Muscle weakness becomes so pronounced that the pupil becomes confined to a wheelchair. This form of the disease is hereditary and is rarely seen in girls.
4. *Spina bifida* is a term that describes a congenital condition that takes a variety of forms. Basically, the disorder is caused by a failure of closure in the spinal column. This damages the spinal cord and nerve roots in a variety of ways and may result in neurological, sensory, and organ problems. Orthopedic care usually begins at birth and continuing physical therapy is often necessary.
5. *Limb deficiencies* may be congenital or acquired after birth. Successful prothesis and adaptability to normal routines are dependent on the location and severity of the loss. Pupils who are handicapped in this way often make excellent adjustments due to he long-standing nature of the condition.

6. *Miscellaneous crippling conditions* result from accidents, both vehicular and home. Included in this category would be instances of child abuse that results in impairment of function. The latter is a situation that will often involve investigation and intervention by members of the pupil services staff.

**Infectious diseases**

These are conditions that may be either acute or chronic depending on time of onset and subsequent treatment. Some may be transmitted in the school situation.

1. *Hepatitis* is manifested by a jaundiced appearance which is caused by swelling and soreness of the liver. It has the highest incidence rate, including all diseases, among children of school.

2. *Nephritis* is seen as puffiness about the eyes and other body parts due to disease of the kidneys. It tends to occur most often in young males.

3. *Mononucleosis* is most prevalent among high school and college age youth. The disease is caused by a virus but can be brought on by fatigue and stress.

**Other health impairments**

1. *Cystic fibrosis* is a hereditary disorder found most often among whites. The condition is characterized by dry coughing and frequent bowel movements. In recent years, medical advances have improved prognosis.

2. Cancer takes the form of leukemia and tumors of the eye, brain, bone, and kidney in children ad youth. The various forms of cancer in children tend to be acute and progress rapidly. Treatment of the disease may result in symptoms like fatigue, weight changes, and nausea. The emotional sequelae may necessitate intervention by pupil services staff.

3. *Asthma* is one of the allergic conditions, often triggered by emotional stress. This illness results in spells of coughing and difficulty in breathing. Although those with mild and moderate involvement will be able to be mainstreamed, there will often be frequent absences from school.
4. *Rheumatic fever* follows a streptococcus infection and is characterized by chronic infection of the connective tissues. Prolonged attacks may result in heart damage. In the latter instance, the pupil services specialist will want to participate in decisions as to program modifications.

In case involving physical disabilities one often encounters the phenomenon of the multiple handicap. Friedman and MacQueen in the survey of physically handicapped school-aged children found that many had secondary handicaps.

> Multihandicapped means concomitant impairments, the combination of which causes such severe educational problems that they cannot be accommodated in special education programs solely for one of the impairments. The term does not include deaf-blind children.

Unfortunately, pupils who are so characterized often find themselves shunted into special education programming based on the primary presenting school-related handicap. This means that if a neurological impairment causes school assessment and performance results that appear to be at the level of mental retardation, this then becomes to replacement. The challenge to the pupil services administrator and staff is to insure that the total pupil is considered in such placement decisions. The parents who have lived with a diagnosis of cerebral palsy from birth do not want school personnel to inform them that the child is mentally retarded. Physical disabilities will often cause secondary handicaps and this should be recognized. Appropriate diagnostic services will probably reveal that there are a number of variables that impact performance. It is short-sighted and less than humanistic to ascribe a handicapping condition to the result of one test score or series of observations.

**The visually impaired**

The visually impaired, frequently listed under the sensorihandicapped, are a group that has captured popular interest. A visual impairment is a malfunction of the eye or optic nerve which prevents normal vision. It is standard practice to define visual impairment by degree of visual acuity and field of vision. The term blindness implied sightlessness but the definition refers to severe limitation in visual functioning. The legally blind are those who have central visual acuity of 20/200 or less in the better eye with correction or whose peripheral field is no grater than 20 degrees. The partially sighted have visual acuity between 20/200 and 20/70 in the better eye. Thus, most legally blind people can see some things but they may look dim, blurred, or out of focus. In addition, they may see only part of an object. The blind usually need braille systems while the partially sighted will require large print books.

It is estimated that approximately 0.1 per cent of school age children are visually handicapped. In translation, this means that a school district population of 5, 000 will have only five pupils so designated. They represent a small number of pupils and according to statistics comprise the smallest group of exceptional children. Etiologically, the visually impaired are the result of events that occurred prior to, during, or shortly after birth. Some have cataracts or retrolental fibroplasia. The diagnosis is usually as follows:

1. Refractive disorder: myopia, hyperopia, cataracts, astigmatism.

2. Muscle disorder: strabismus, nystagmus, amblyopia.
3. Receptive disorder: retrolental fibroplasia, optic atrophy.

**Instructional provisions**

Over the years, instruction for the physically disabled has moved increasingly from the hospital to the school setting. In the school setting, as a result of P.L. 94-142, there is also movement from the self-contained special class to the specially adapted regular classroom. In perhaps no other exceptionalitly is the need for multidisciplinary planning so crucial. The team may frequently involve specialists from social work, psychology, speech therapy, nursing, rehabilitation counseling, and physical and occupational therapy, nursing, rehabilitation counseling, and physical ad occupational therapy as well as recreation. Whereas the other handicapping conditions involve essentially mental and emotional components, the physically disabled subpopulation will often entail these in combination with physical limitations. In many school districts, this range of services may not be readily available; therefore, these services must be rendered on a consultative basis. Providing for the full range of services poses a particular problem for the pupil services administrator. However, once the team is assembled, there should be a focus on four developmental goals.

1. Physical independence, including mastery of daily-living skills.
2. Self-awareness and social maturation.
3. Academic growth.
4. Career education, including constructive leisure activities.

These components should become an integral part of the Individualized Education Program. The team will be assisted by the parents in the development of the IEP, an ingredient that was lacking in the pre-P.L. 94-142 era. There is probably nothing more important to the physically disabled pupil than physical independence. It has been noted that one of the prime targets for professional personnel is to move the physically disabled person from dependence to independence. Not surprisingly, one of the cornerstones of independence is freedom of physical movement from place to place. If one must depend on others for daily living activities, it is bound to foster dependence or frustration in the best adjusted person. Key personnel in the attainment of physical independence are physical and occupational therapists. The importance of occupational therapy is specified in the 1977 P.L-142 regulations under related services.

Occupational therapy includes

1. Improving, developing, or restoring functions impaired or lost through illness, injury, or deprivation.
2. Improving ability to perform tasks for independent functioning when functions are impaired or lost.
3. Preventing, through early intervention, initial or further impairment or loss of function.

Prior to the advent of P.L. 94-142, these services were rarely seen in the schools. Physical ad occupational therapists have been traditionally hospital-bound personnel and individuals have been referred to these settings for evaluation and treatment. This still obtains for only a limited number of school districts employ physical and occupational therapists. However, more are being hired on a consultative basis to serve the schools. One of the persistent problems for the pupil services administrator is to locate such personnel for employment particularly if the district is removed from metropolitan areas or areas that have comprehensive medical facilities. In the attainment of physical independence during the school hours, there is need for adaptive physical sites, equipment, and materials. The emphasis in the Rehabilitation Act of 1973, P.L. 93-112, Second 504, has increased sensitivity to barrier-free locations but adaptive equipment ad materials remain the responsibility of educators who wish to implement least restrictive environments. Although not all locations have to be adapted, most existing buildings with heavy concentrations of physically disabled pupils could make modest modifications without exorbitant costs. A partial list of some minor changes is as follows:

1. Ramps as well as steps for wheelchairs and crutches.
2. Handbars by drinking fountains, toilet stalls, and blackboards
3. Removal of desks to make room for a wheelchair.
4. Modification of furniture to provide for the pupil with braces.
5. Rubber mats over slippery floors.
6. Wide doorways.

While only a general statement can be made about the adaptation of equipment and materials, there should be available to the teaching staff a variety of devices to meet individual pupil needs. Each disability, or combination of disabilities, requires its own adaptations. Some of these adaptations are as follows:

1. Availability of pencil-holding devices or other modification of pencils to assist holding.
2. Provision of trays to keep pencil and crayons from falling to the floor.

3. Provision of book holders or mechanical page turns.
4. Modification of electric typewriters with cutouts for keys.
5. Installation of foot rests.

Some of these approaches may seem minor, but sometimes small steps taken toward the achievement of independence can lead to greater self-confidence and a desire for more physical independence.

**Social, academic and career development**

In terms of *self-awareness and social maturation* nothing is more important than the development of a positive self-concept. The development of a positive self-concept may be difficult because the physical disability can engender feelings of inadequacy and insecurity. In addition, the physically impaired pupil may experience an attitude of rejection from parents and peers. Not only is self-concept derived from interactions with others but from self-image which, in turn, may be influenced by body image. In essence, the physically disabled pupil must be assisted of feel good about himself or herself which can lead to self-awareness and social maturation. Physically disabled pupils will have their share of adjustment problems but there is nothing in the literature to indicate that this subpopulation is automatically maladjusted. Meyerson states that the physically disabled may be more vulnerable to emotional disturbance than the non-disabled for two reasons:

1. Being placed in more "new" situations than their non-disabled counterparts.
2. Being forced to live in overlapping psychological worlds-one for the disabled and the other for the "normal".

Meyerson suggests solutions to these problems (1) lie

in increasing frustration tolerance and teaching adaptation skills and (2) reducing pressure that cause one to seek inaccessible and unobtainable goals that tend to exclude. Certainly, the physically disabled must learn more about their potential and limitations so that coping mechanisms can be at their highest level. As part of the self-awareness process, physically disabled pupils must be assisted in the exploration of feelings sot that they can deal with both frustration and criticism. *Academic growth* is important because, as previously pointed out, the physically disabled as a group tend to be educationally deficient. If a pupil loses much time for school it may be necessary to offer tutorial instruction. Obviously, comprehensive diagnostic assessment is necessary in order to determine educational and sensory deficits. However, the curricular approach to the physically disabled must be flexible in the realization that some pupils, particularly at the secondary level, must learn survival skills. Individual academic growth will be facilitated by the new electronic technology which will provide support for missing or defective body parts as well as sensory and motor deficits. Individualization of instruction will revolve around the IEP and annual growth will be charted and monitored through this vehicle. The pupil services specialist should be alert to the need for innovative approaches to the instruction of the physically disabled. Beyond this the pupil services specialist should ensure that needs and strategies are introduced at the team meeting. In this endeavor he or she must have the active support of the pupil services administrator for there is apt to be resistance to such suggestions on the grounds of time and costs. Pupil services staff will be reluctant to assume an activist stance in these matters without administrative support.

The area of *career education* received heavy emphasis during the 1970s in the schools with all subpopulations.

By the midseventies, there was an awareness that this concept should also be applied to the handicapped. It is particularly relevant for the physically handicapped because over the years they have been systematically excluded from a variety of options in the work place. Related to career education is career education, career development cannot take place. What has hampered the career development of the physically disabled is the presence of stereotypes that the general public, and perhaps, the physically disabled themselves believe. These stereotypes have been summarized by Osipow. A discussion of stereotypical assumptions about the disabled have also been discussed by Beane and Zachmanoglou and Humes. Stereotypes must be combated because they tend to be internalized by the physically handicapped and result in self-fulfilling prophecies. The starting point for comprehensive career development is a sequential, systematic program of career education. Career education is intended to help the handicapped as well as the nonhandicaped. There are five psychosocial components to career education and they all have relevance for the disabled.

1. Career education assists individuals in becoming aware of the relationship between their maturity and their evolving aspirations, values, and potentialities.
2. Career education assists individuals in developing a sense of worth, purpose, and direction in life.
3. Career education assists the individual in becoming a part of rather than apart from society. This sense of participation leads to direct application of the principles of normalization.
4. Career education provides the individual with the security of legitimation in relation to the norms of achieving adult status.

5. Career education enables individuals to become fully capacitated to perform all of life's role more effectively.

*Carrer development in the Nonhandicapped and handicapped*

| *Assumptions About Career Development in the Nonhandicapped* | *Assumptions About Career Development in the Handicapped* |
|---|---|
| 1. Career development is systematic. | 1. Career development is unsystematic, i.e., the handicapped had better take what it available. |
| 2. Career development is psychologically influenced | 2. Career development is not psychological since the handicapped don't have much psychological life. |
| 3. Carrier development is a major force in | 3. Career development one's life is not important for the handicapped. |
| 4. The total person is involved in career development. | 4. The handicap overrides other characteristics in determining career behaviour. |
| 5. People are multipotential in careers. | 5. The career options of the handicapped are very limited. |
| 6. Career behaviour is developmental | 6. The career development of the handicapped is arrested or retarded. |
| 7. Career development is stressful at choice | 7. The career development of the handicapped is stressful at all points. |

At the same time that career education is going on, there is a concurrent growth in career development.

Career development of the physically disabled should have as its goal the "preparation for all meaningful ad productive activity, at work or at leisure, whether paid or volunteer, as employee and employer, in private business or in the public sector, or in the family". Career development activities for the physically disabled should have a K-12 emphasis. At the secondary level, a period of exploration should embrace the following elements.

1. Exposure to occupational information via lectures, books, pamphlets, films, and filmstrips, and multimedia kits. Occupationally field trips and resource speakers afford excellent opportunities for the student both to acquire occupational information and to become aware of work opportunities available in the community.
2. Exposure to physically disabled adults representative of a wide variety of semiskilled, skilled and professional occupations.
3. Exposure to job-related equipment and devices that can assist a physically disabled individual in overcoming his/her physical limitations. Ideally the exposure should include opportunities to (a) observe others use these devices and (b) engage in "hands-on" experience in the classroom, vocational or scientific laboratory, or at the work site of a disabled person.
4. Opportunity to acquire knowledge about one's occupational interests, strength, and weaknesses via comprehensive educational-occupational assessment that should include work samples and/or other forms of simulated work experiences.
5. Opportunities to participate in a wide variety of a academic-occupational classroom, laboratory, and work-training experiences. It is especially important

that the physically disabled not be arbitrarily excluded from such "nonacademic" subjects as art and music, physical education, laboratory science, and homemaking/industrial education at either the elementary or secondary level. For some of the more severely disabled individuals, specially organized classes or an individualized program in these subjects may be needed. Supervised work experience also is important for the physically disabled since they typically have more difficulty than the able-bodied in obtaining part-time or summer employment.

Characteristic of many of the physically disabled reflect the absence of work-related and social experiences that are part of the every day lives of the nondisabled adolescent. These experience deficits put the physically disabled at a severe disadvantage in relationship to their nondisabled counterparts. Some of the physically disabled have been so sheltered that they do not realize that lower echelon jobs usually precede higher level responsibilities ad that one earns vacation time only after a period of successful employment. Pupil services workers should not take for granted the existence of back-ground and experience that contribute to an understanding of the work world.

The aforementioned goals, while not all-inclusive, should provide a blue-print for pupil services workers and administrators as they approach the delicate task of providing an appropriate educational experience for physically disabled pupils. Developmental goals such as these must be believed and subscribed to by those who promote them. To this extent, pupil services specialists and administrators must examine their own attitude toward the physically disabled.

**Counseling the physically disabled**

Counselling strategies with the physically disable

not be markedly dissimilar from those used with the nondisabled. Client-centered, behavioural, and cognitive-oriented techniques may be equally applicable depending on the pupil, counselor, and setting. It is important that the counselor know something about the nature of physical disabilities ad have some coursework or practical experiences. As an entry point the counselor must be cognizant of some of the characteristics of the physically disabled. They are as follows:

1. Many have had few of the social experiences and as a result may be immature and lacking in self-confidence.
2. Some will have aspirations that are too low, while others may have aspirations that are much too high.
3. Many will be reluctant to trust their own judgment and will be sell inclined to take on a planning role.
4. Much of career planning may be unrealistic or stereotypic.
5. Many will focus on their limitations rather than abilities.
6. Some will feel that educational weaknesses are due to mental limitation rather than lack of opportunity.

The counselor in assisting physically disabled pupils must be oriented to individual coping levels particularly as they affect career and vocational issues. The coping levels must zero in on the areas of work-accessibility, work performance, and work rewards. Various questions must be posed by the counselor both to himself or herself and to the counselee. However, in order to make the counseling process meaningful, the pupil must assume a participatory stance in order to resolve the questions. The physically disabled are so conditioned to having things done to them or for them that it is difficult to reverse this expectation and assume responsibility for their own actions. The ultimate goals is to permit the physically disabled to assume responsibility for their own lives. However, this cannot happen unless all avenues and opportunities have been made available at the appropriate time and place.

*Attitudes toward physical disability*

One of the problems facing the pupil services administrator and staff deals with attitudes of the nondisabled toward disabled peers. As pointed out by Siller, most individuals coming into interaction with the physically disabled feel anxiety or even a version. Numerous studies can be quoted to confirm that physically disabled persons are often regarded less favourably than the nondisabled. One can reasonably expect this range of feelings from the regular education staff. If the teaching corps cannot view the disabled in a reasonably positive fashion, one can expect a limited range of interest at the IEP team meetings. Modification of such negative attitudinal components involves the necessity of comprehensive staff development ad in-service efforts. A number of techniques have been used to produce positive attitudinal changes toward the physically disabled. They can be placed in categories as follows:

1. Director or indirect contacts between the disabled and nondisabled.
2. Provision of information about disabilities.
3. Persuasion and exhortation.
4. Analysis of the roots of prejudice.
5. Simulation exercises.
6. Discussion in groups.

Some of the techniques are not effective than others. One

of the more successful is actual contact but it works best in structured situations when the participants have equal status. Mere information and persuasion have a limited effect. Any effort to produce attitudinal change should be spearheaded by the pupil services administrator by virtue of his knowledge about the dimensions of the problem. In planning such programs the administrator should remember the following:

1. Attitudinal components toward the physically disabled can be identified and measured.
2. A generalization of attitude components appears to exist across all disabilities.
3. The separate components of attitude within physical disability are positively correlated.
4. Demographic variables are important in the way that attitudes are expressed.
5. Negative attitudinal components are recognized by persons holding to them.

One may expect negative attitudes in some pupil services staff and even in some pupil services administrators When these occur, it will undoubtedly be necessary to provide intensive and well-organized seminars, for the feelings may be deep and not readily retrievable. The pupil services administrator with negative attitudes will have to work especially hard to bring the reasons for the devaluation to awareness. In dealing with the physically disabled a method of work sampling is crucial if the pupil services worker is to have some direction for training and placement. Work sampling is particularly important when the vocational prospects for the pupil are not clearly evident. Work sampling or assessment can be accomplished in on-job-training or in workshop settings. The objective is to expose the pupil to a variety of work stations where practical job skills can be demonstrated. Work station experiences can include paper-and-pencil tests, commercial exercises, or job simulations with step-by-step instructions. In work sampling experiences in workshop or rehabilitation settings it is customary to use one of a variety of commercially produced work sample packages. Among them are:

1. *Jewish Employment and Vocational Service System:* Measures potential in industrial categories and includes 28 work samples for hands-on assessment of skills, behaviour, and interests. Work activities of assembly/disassembly, binding, clerical, display/printing, electrical, mail handling, structural development, and metal work are included.
2. *Testing, Orientation, and Work Evaluation in Rehabilitation:* Is the oldest and perhaps best-known work sample system for the disabled. Consists of 94 work samples clustered into 14 occupational areas. Work activities include jewelry manufacturing, drafting, drawing, sewing, and electronics assembly. Personality dimensions of work habits, work tolerance, attitudes, speed, and motivation are also assessed.
3. *Social and Prevocational Information Battery:* Developed for use with retarded individuals and includes knowledge areas in employability, economic self-sufficiency, family living, personal habits, and communication.
4. *Singer Vocational Evaluation System:* An audiovisual approach to work activities in areas of bench assembly, electrical wiring, plumbing and pipe-fitting, cooking and baking, and cosmetology.
5. *Valpar Component Work Sample System:* Has 16 individual assessment units which have been standardized for both able bodied workers and the physically disabled. Units measure skills of size

discrimination, clerical comprehension and aptitude, independent problem-solving, eye-hand-foot coordination, and money handling.

There is no one group that will need and receive more counseling and support assistance than the emotionally troubled. Assistance will be rendered along the entire spectrum of the handicap and will include those who are designated as emotionally disturbed and eligible for special education. The need for counseling or therapeutic intervention with this subpopulation is greater than for any other. The stakes are not only immediate but life-long. According to Dimick and Huff the lack of intervention with those who have emotional problems will result in more disabilities than all other health conditions in combination. This is most surprising when one considers that success of failure in life is contingent on an individuals' reservoir of adaptive responses. Counseling activities with the emotionally handicapped may be either indirect or direct. Pupils being treated therapeutically by outside practitioners will usually be seen by a pupil services specialist in only a consultative or liaison role. On the other hand, pupils with mild handicapping conditions may have no other service but other service but the efforts of the school counselor, school psychologist, school social worker, and so forth. Eyde has developed a descriptive figure which relates the level of emotional handicap to degrees of counseling involvement.

1. *Severe disorder*: This is the group of emotionally handicapped pupils who fit the P.L. 94-142 definition of "severely emotionally disturbed". These pupils will, and should be treated by psychiatrists, clinical psychologists, or mental health treatment teams. The pupil services specialist will generally perform a liaison function between the outside clinical service and the school. It is a rule of thumb that counseling

within the school will not take place simultaneously with treatment rendered by an outside source.

2. *Moderate diorder*: Pupils within this grouping may be in a resource room situation or in regular classes. It is practically certain that these pupils will require counseling from either outside sources or school personnel. If counseling takes place within the confines of the school, there may be need of a counseling IEP. These pupils may manifest conflicts in the areas of affect, anxiety, and impulse control.

3. *Mild diorder*: This relatively large group comprise the group who will remain in the regular classroom. They may not qualify for special educational services but will yet appear emotionally troubled. The pupil services workers' role will be consultant to the teacher in the realm of classroom management. It is likely that most referrals will come from impulse control management. It is likely that most referrals will come from impulse control problems which will be shown through disruptive behavior and aggressive reactions.

4. *Marginal adjustment:* The marginally adjusted pupil is the one who can benefit from preventive measures. The pupil services worker, and specifically the school counselor, serves as a developmental specialist for this group of pupils. The counselor will often alert both the teacher and home about a potential problem that may be avoided through the structuring of learning experiences.

5. *Sound mental health*: The pupil services specialist may focus on the developmental needs of the "normal" population and will function essentially as a mental health educator. The pupil services specialist will endeavor to promote group and individual activities which will reinforce sound mental health. The pupil

services worker will also attempt to develop an ecosystem that will be conducive to sound mental health. With this group the staff member functions as a curricular adviser, teacher trainer, and parent educator.

Along this spectrum of degree of handicap the pupil services administrator may see the opportunity to parcel out areas of responsibility so that territorial concerns are minimal. The school counselor would have prime responsibility for those with sound mental health, marginal adjustment, and mild disorders. The school psychologist and school social worker would have principal responsibility for dealing with those pupils who manifest moderate and severe disorders. Naturally, this division of labor will be dependent on availability of staffing and philosophy of the district.

**Indirect and direct services**

It is possible to identify three supportive counseling services for the pupil services worker which can be considered indirect services. These are consultation, collaboration, and conceptualization. The consultant attempts to achieve a match between the pupils' developmental needs and the learning environments. In order to serve as an effective consultant to the providers of instructional services to the emotionally handicapped the pupil services workers must deal with issues of lack of information, lack of skills, lack of confidence, and lack of objectivity. As *collaborator* the pupil services specialist will assist in the coordination of IEPs which for the emotionally handicapped pupil will probably involve considerable contact with regular classroom teachers due to the fact that may of these pupils will be mainstreamed. The pupil services specialist as *conceptulizer* is somewhat more difficult to delineate because it entails observation of the total or "big" picture and reaching some conclusion as to what may be the cause or cure of an individual or institutional problems. If the conceptualizer role does not fall to the pupil services specialist, it may fall to no one. The conceptualizer must determine what areas are impacting the pupil, whether school, home, or community, and how these forces may be modified.

Direct services may include behavioral change counseling, biofeedback training, life-space interviewing, affective education classes, leisure education and therapeutic play, peer counseling, and parent education. The latter is a particularly useful form of counseling to ameliorate the problems of the emotionally handicapped. It has been often observed that part of many emotional disturbance situations is a disordered parent-child relationship. If parents can understand their own adjustment problems, the dynamics of the home situation may change and in so doing the interactions with the pupil may improve. All direct services with emotionally handicapped pupils and their families require special personal qualities and personal commitments. Establishing a relationship and conveying a sense of caring is a must. Typically, the emotionally handicapped pupil and his/her parents have felt frustrated, neglected, isolated, and misunderstood. In order to overcome these feelings of rejection it is necessary to focus on the individual rather than the problem. It is not easy to work with those who experience emotional problems. Those who need the most help often engage in self-defeating behavior in an effort to reinforce feelings of self-rejection and to encourage hostility on the part of those who seek to help. It goes without saying that every pupil services specialist is not equipped to engage in direct services with this subpopulation.

**Development and administration problems**

Next to learning disabilities the emotionally handicapped represent the newest category. As such it is still in a process of growth and redefinition. While P.L. 94-142 served to delimit the number of pupils who could be so categorized, it remains a fact that the emotionally troubled are still out there. They must be served, either through special education avenues or some modification thereof. It remains the category of most concern to teachers and administrators because of the daily challenged posed by this subpopulation. Some of the issues to be dealt with by a pupil services administrator will be discussed in further detail.

**Role of support personnel**

An issue of considerable interest to pupil services administrators and staff is the role of support personnel in identification, placement, and follow-up of the emotionally handicapped. The pupil services specialist is usually the first person, after the initial referral, who sees the pupil suspected of being emotionally disturbed. Undoubtedly, the pupil has emotional problems, as perceived by another person, but the task of the pupil services worker is to conduct an initial "screening" to determine whether the pupil is within normal limits in terms of adaptive behavior. Such screening will depend on may situational variables, for example, adequacy and philosophy of the district, competency of the teaching staff, socioeconomic climate of the school, and so forth. Accordingly, it is not as simplistic as many classroom teachers and general administrators would like it to be. The pupil services worker must make a decision either to go forward with diagnostic instrumentation, a costly procedure, or refer back to the teacher. Unfortunately, the initial introduction is judge like in nature, a heavy role indeed. This role will be especially difficult in small schools or districts where the pupil services worker cannot talk with colleagues about prediagnostic impressions. During the placement or IEP process the pupil services specialist who reviewed and prepared the case materials will be expected to make a recommendation based on diagnostic impressions. This will probably be easiest for the school psychologist, due to the availability of test instrumentation, but even here the problem is exacerbated by the fact that test instrumentation is imprecise in terms of diagnosis of emotional disturbance. Once a pupil is placed, there is more need for follow up of the emotional handicapped than for any of the other subpopulations because emotional handicaps are dynamic and reversible. If possible, a pupil service worker should remain in contact with every pupil who has been designated as emotionally handicapped and determined by the IEP team to be in need of special education. If there are staff shortages the pupil services administrator must try to design alternative strategies to make the consultive approach work. Adul education programs might be considered as an alternative.

**Diagnosis**

Related to the role of support personnel is the question of diagnosis. The federal IEP regulations are quite specific as to who should be classified as "severely emotionally disturbed". Should such a classification be assigned by a group of school professionals, based on demonstrated behavior, or should the designation be reserved for clinic personnel? The answer rests, in part, on whether one chooses to follow an educational or medical model. It is possible to mount compelling arguments on both sides. While the education model will tend to move pupils in and out of special education programs more readily, clinical diagnosis is more apt to result in treatment and parental acceptance. If a given district chooses to use a categorical model, it may be expeditious to utilize outside clinical personnel for consensual validation. The designation "emotional disturbance" is a heavy label to assign to any pupil for it may convey more to the parent, community, and society than school staff intend. For example, there is evidence that behavioral disorders have both a sexual and racial bias in that minority males are often overrepresented. Conversely, it has been suggested that the moderately disturbed child is being denied services due to regulatory exclusion.

**Negative Stereotypes**

While it is debatable as to whether emotional disturbance or mental retardation has the most negative image, there is no doubt that emotional disturbance is a label that few people cover for a pupil. The label suggests disordered and unacceptable behavior that is a threat to others. From a parental point of view, it is usually construed as an indictment of the parent-child relationship. The negative stereotypes associated with this handicap have prevented many pupils from getting needed help. In most districts, IEP teams must either label or describe behavior before goals and objectives can be finalized. In the process such labeling or description of behavior must be interpreted to parents who may have habituated an avoidance mechanism. In recognition of this eventuality, a pupil services specialist may decide not to label or describe the pupils as "seriously emotionally disturbed" for fear that the parents will reject the diagnosis and withdraw support of any treatment and placement considerations. In many districts attempts have been made to devise a short-form of the IEP so that parents will not have to face the narration of the uncomfortable details of a full-blown disturbance. The pupil services administrator must seek ways to make an emotional handicap more respectable and palatable. Such strategies may include parent seminars, teacher in-service programs, and pupil self-awareness.

**Juvenile Delinquency**

There is mounting evidence that juvenile delinquents have a high incidence of learning disabilities. This finding is remarkable only in that it took so long to establish the linkage. Juvenile offenders are typically school failures and early dropouts. Aside from other socioeconomic factors these youth obviously never found learning to be either relevant or simple. Certainly, the likelihood of school failure can lead to emotional problems and-depending on intrapsychic, family, and community pressures-can precipitate juvenile delinquency. Although juvenile offenders are hardly a homogeneous group, a large measure of hostility may be expressed in socially unacceptable ways. These are the "acting out" pupils who plague the lives of many teachers. Such pupils will be a constant source of referrals to pupil services staff. In order to deal with the phenomenon the pupil services worker will have to assume a change-agent role. That is, there must be a recognition that many of the causes are alloplastic in nature which necessitate going to the community or family for modifications in the environment. The high dropout rate with this subpopulation indicates the need for more intensive effort in the area of primary prevention.

**Mainstreaming**

It is a truism that most emotionally troubled youth will be served in the regular classroom by regular teachers. A relative handful will be categorized as emotionally disturbed and therefore eligible for special education of some kind. Those who remain in regular classrooms will continue to be troubled or to trouble teaching staffs. Pupils who are not designated as in need of special education will probably received no extra assistance unless pupil service specialists choose to intervene. Such intervention will support the regular class placement and may involve counseling, consultation, community mobilization, and the like. In such situations no team meetings are required nor is an IEP necessary. On the surface, this procedure would seem to make the possibility of service more flexible and less bound to bureaucratic restrictions. However, the pupil service specialist will be under great pressure to serve first those who have an IEP. By virtue of traditional job roles intervention can probably best be carried out by the school counselor. The school counselor, serving the developmental needs of *all* youth, is nor restricted by special education parameters. The concept of mainstreaming does receive a lot of publicity and was in the forefront of special education thinking even before P. L. 94-142 was enacted. When it has succeeded, it has usually been through the efforts of special education teachers and a selected few regular education teachers. There is evidence that pupil services workers and special education teachers are more in agreement on behavioral objectives for this subpopulation than regular class teachers.

### Need for more service

A recent report by the Children's Defense Fund indicates that two-thirds of the nations' seriously emotionally disturbed pupils are not receiving appropriate special education and related services. The researchers for the Fund, an advocacy group, reviewed the statutes and litigation involving emotionally disturbed children and adolescents and reached the following conclusions:

1. Implementation has been hindered by confusion about how severe a disturbance must be to be covered by the regulations;
2. The schools' responsibility for psychotherapy, often a needed adjunct service, remains unclear;
3. Resistance to the obligation to pay for residential treatment, when needed, where documented by the schools inability to provide;

4. School psychologists spend practically all their time testing and do not have enough time left for counseling pupils and consulting with teachers;
5. Emphasis on serving the seriously emotionally disturbed has reduced mental health intervention strategies for early attention;
6. Some school are not referring emotionally disturbed pupils for services;
7. States have been remiss in not encouraging the development of training programs to increase the pool of qualified teachers.

The need for counseling is obvious when one is aware that early recipients of learning disabilities services were found to need supportive ad vocational assistance as adults. Practically all pupil services specialists may become involved in counseling SLD pupils. Counseling has proven effective with this subpopulation. Due to the fact that behavioural and adjustment problems often overlap cognitive deficits, there is a need for the counselor to deal with coping and self-control skills. In dealing with these strategies, the helper may choose to use either a counseling or consultation model. In addition to the student, the counselor will work with the teacher(s) and parent(s).

Students with long standing SLD problems will demonstrate a variety of behavioural symptoms, chief among them will be low self-esteem, anxiety, anger and frustration. Counseling strategies which apply particularly to the adolescent, should:

1. Offer a chance for success, no matter how small.
2. Build an inclination to try by structuring small segments of assigned tasks.
3. Minimize situations where threats, punishment, and strong reactions of adults are prevalent.

4. Keep the student to a reasonable time schedule once he begin to make progress.
5. Ally deep-seated fears that he is somehow mentally subnormal.

Counselors who deal with students who have ambivalence over intelligence may find it useful to use Lloyd Thompson's entitled "Language Disabilities in men of Eminence". In this provocative piece, Thompson uses a psychohistorical approach to illustrate that some great men in history probably had SLD. Among the people described are Thomas Edison, Harvey Cushing, Auguste Rodin, George Patton, Woodrow Wilson, Paul Ehrlich, Albert Einstein and George Washington. Adolescents can identify with these eminent people and realize that all is not necessarily lost because one had a learning problem in school.

Counseling techniques will differ on the basis of specific problem behaviour. However, Edge, Brown, and Brown suggest some that may be generally applicable.

1. For inadequacy, try "strength bombardment" in a group setting.
2. For anxiety, try relaxation training.
3. For anger, try a cognitive approach, perhaps rational-emotive counselling, or "I messages."
4. For frustration or inappropriate interactions try "time out".

There is also need for parent and family counseling. Stress and sibling rivalry are commonly found in families of learning-disabled students "parents feel ambivalence guilt, fear...but... must always subside to the reality that theirs is still a handicapped child who seems normal, but doesn't appear to learn and/or behave normally". This is the essence of the parental frustration, namely, trying to understand how a child who is normal in most ways can fail to learn in school, even with massive amounts of tutoring and family support.

**Career preparation and developscareer development.** As is true with most mildly handicapped adolescents, the youth who make up this subpopulation will most likely enter the competitive work force after graduation from high school. Of course, some will advance to higher education but it is apparent that an academically delimiting handicap like SLD will dictate circumscribed horizons. Too little attention has been paid heretofore to the postsecondary future of the SLD pupil. Part of the problem is related to the difference between career and vocational education/development. Vocational development has a narrower focus and in terms of special education populations has tended to emphasize a limited clientele. Vocational education programs, albeit sorely limited in some parts of the country, have been targeted primarily at those pupils in some parts of the country, have been targeted primarily at those pupils categorized as educable mentally retarded. This targeting developed, in part, from the belief that the mildly retarded had very few choices. The learning-disabled, however, comprise a heterogeneous group with much broader options. Accordingly, the concepts of career preparation and development are highly applicable. If a career is the totality of work or activities over a life time, then a more comprehensive approach is necessary with SLD pupils. However, before strategies are instituted there must be a realization that the SLD pupil required career development assistance.

Due to the fact that the SLD pupil has the given of "normal" intelligence it is often assumed that he or she can move through the secondary school situation in lockstep with nonhandicapped pupils. The implication is that SLD pupils will somehow absorb incidental career information that will be self-utilized upon graduation. While this rationale is difficult, at best, for even the nonhandicapped pupil it is disastrous for the SLD pupil. A SLD pupil is typically exerting every ounce of energy to survive the academic demands of the secondary school. If one accepts this restraint it is easy to see why little attention will be given to incidental types of learning that are part of the repertoire of informal career preparation and development. Bingham has observed that boys with SLD are less mature in their responses on the Carrier Maturity Index and require planned experience to develop vocational maturity. Kendall found that subjects enrolled in vocational-training classes were superior in social maturity and career attitudes.

Another hurdle for school counselors who are concerned with career development is the often unreasonable expectations of the parents. This "hidden handicap" will sometimes lead parents astray and arouse expectations of educational and occupational choices that are far beyond the proven capabilities the SLD pupil. This can be a particular problem for youth who come from college-educated or professional families. Although some youth have internalized these parental expectation, most will feel relieved to be guided toward more realistic choices. An additional variable is the actual range of possibilities that may be available. IT has been pointed out previously that some colleges are now opening their doors to the identified learning-disabled motivated, successfully-coping pupil. However, the range of possibilities between vocation and college education is much less appealing. Technical schools and related occupations have yet to feel the need to adapt to the needs of the learning-disabled.

The pupil services administrator and staff must be alert to the need for career preparation and development for the SLD adolescent at these times. If quantity and quality of academic programming were the issues of the seventies then postsecondary career issues will be the frontier of the eighties. It should be reiterated that P.L. 93-112, the Rehabilitation Act of 1973, does recognize specific learning disabilities as an adult disorder. The SLD person is entitled to the same considerations as others with more visible handicaps. The pupil services staff must forge a linkage with rehabilitation counselors and employers. This is a task that will fall to school counselors, school psychologists, and school social workers.

**Development and administration problems**

There are a number of issues conforming the pupil service administrator within the domains of both development and management. The problems may differ depending on the maturity of the department, but the problem areas have similarities. An initial development problem centres around the instructional delivery system that is best for the district and the student configuration. For example, is it better to go with a tutoring program as opposed to the resources room concept? Once a procedure has been initiated, it is difficult, but not impossible, to change. The pupil services administrator must examine the nature of the SLD staff/parental expectations and financial resources and act accordingly. A development or redevelopment should utilize the needs-assessment technique so all parties are in agreement. Another development issue to be faced in the 1980s is when expansion should cease. During the 1970s the objective was to increase services so as to meet the needs of an unserved population. The time will come when not only will it be appropriate to limit expansion but also to reduce services. At a time when general school enrollments are decreasing and regular class teachers are being dismissed, can one in good conscience continue SLD services at the same level? This issue must be resolved through analysis of caseloads and the generation of "hard data" for justification. Specific management problems may revolve around the maintenance of identification standards, standardization of caseloads, interstaff relationships, least restrictive environment, and evaluation/accountability.

**Maintenance of identified standards**

As the nationwide concern for specific learning disabilities has increased, it was inevitable that more mild conditions would be included. There are many pupils in school with learning problems and some may have some of the characteristics associated with definitions of SLD. The issue for a pupil services administrator is whether such pupils are eligible for special education. Gearheart recognizes this issue but believes that preventive efforts may be one of the most effective ways to deliver learning disabilities programming. Others would agree that prevention is the best way to approach any emerging disability but might quarrel with the designation of the delivery system. The instruction of mild cases, which may not meet formal identification criteria, might properly belong in the domains of remedial or compensatory education. A pragmatic view would hold that the pupil should receive service wherever it is available, with the recognition that the budget climate of the eighties is not conducive to either the establishment or maintenance of nonspecial education programming. The team, whether by school or district, will decide who is eligible for services and the pupil services administrator must exercise leadership in developing a philosophical point of view as to what constitutes a specific learning disability which, in turn, will influence standards. The problem for the pupil services administrator is no an easy one, for it involves a number of variables differing from district to district. Some of the questions that can be posed are:

1. Will the dilution of standards eventually do more harm than good by resulting in reduction for funding brought on by greater numbers?
2. If some kind of service is provided, even if not condoned by the regulations, will it eventually reduce the prevalence of SLD?
3. Should the broad range of learning problems be served, from whatever source, for the grater good of society?

***Standardization of caseloads***

A building-oriented approach to specific learning disabilities is becoming standard in many parts of the country due both to the ubiquitous nature of SLD and to the fact that it is often the preferred choice of most general administrators and parents. That there is no threat or stigma to having an SLD center in a given school contributes to its desirability and popularity. As this development occurs, SLD teacher who are completely building-based become increasingly under the jurisdiction of building principals. There is nothing wrong with this traditional supervisory model nit it presents a problem to the pupil services administrator because principals tend to view services from a different perspective. As building managers, principals are under pressures different from those of central office administrators. Principals, unlike most pupil services administrators, have a constituency that is composed of the parents and/or pupils of the entire school. Accordingly, the principal as to meet the demands of the constituency in terms of services. If remedial services in the school are limited or nonexistent, he/she may be inclined to request services from the SLD center even though a pupil may not have yet cleared a team meeting or, at best, is marginally eligible. The motivation in such requests is usually commendable and eminently pupil-centered so the principal cannot be faulted on help-giving grounds. Naturally, such requests are difficult if not impossible to deny for a building-based special education teacher. As a result caseloads in individual schools may vary widely, sometimes from 15-30 pupils per teacher. When such a discrepancy is revealed it causes a furor among special education teachers and parents. It is the responsibility of the pupil services administrator to insure that standard caseloads are observed both for quality of service and staff morale. To his extent, it is advisable to have an approved policy statement on record to indicate minimum and maximum pupil limits. Once these and similar questions are addressed the pupil services administrator may determine if the standards are set, it is certain that they will not be popular with all segments of the administrator's constituency, whether other administrators, teachers, pupil services staff, or parents. Therefore, in trying to modify or maintain standards, the administrator will have to use all the managerial skills at his/her command.

*Interstaff relationships*

Relationships among SLD teachers, psychologists, speech-language pathologists, and social workers often need improvement. Specifically, the different specialities sometimes are at variance with regard to the identification and instructional needs of those pupils who are described as learning-disabled. This kind of intergroup conflict seems to occur with the SLD population more than with other exceptionalities. It is due, in part, to the nebulous quality of the handicap but, in addition, it reflects the compelling need of all specialists to get involved in program planning. All have a take in the IEP whether by virtue of professional identity, administrative requirements, or parental expectations. Due to "turf" issues interstaff relationships often deteriorate and assume conflict proportions. For a host of reasons, among them being popularity and acceptance, most staff members want to participate in SLD program planning and development. It is probably crucial that IEP meetings be attended by representatives of all the disciplines. This is a good strategy because no one specialty will feel slighted or left out. The essence here is participation and not necessarily decision making. Another potent device is to involve all disciplines in policy-making decisions that affect the SLD subpopulation. Noninvolvement can lead to feelings or rejection, frustration, and hostility. Another technique is to involve all specialities in any efforts at parent education. With regard to SLD it is expedient to allow each specialty to become identified with SLD in the parents' minds. The parental lobby in specific learning disabilities has been a powerful one and this has not been lost on pupil services staff. The hidden agenda here is that if programs are expanded, usually at the behest of parents, then all specialities should have an opportunity to partake of the largesse.

***Least restrictive environment***

Nowhere is the debate about the least restrictive environment more intense than in the arena of specific learning disabilities. Support and arguments run the gamut from advocates of total normalization to the need for private school placement. It is possible to make a case for his range of placements as it is for no other exceptionality. Normalization or mainstreaming is not always successful because it is often administratively inspired and a "competency-based assessment" has been suggested. P.L. 94-142 leans a variety of ways. An activist parents of a severely learning-disabled adolescent will often see least restriction being offered in a residential private school pectations of public school personnel. Similarly, a school social worker might see the same pupil as requiring contact with normal environment sot that "them" arrangement. Sometimes, representatives of the "us,"-namely, school personnel-become advocates for the parent posture which presents an interesting loyalty dilemma. The pupil services administrator must deal with this explosive issue, which represents one of the persistent challenges. First, the pupil services administrator must campaign actively for a true continuum of environments within the school district so that parents can perceive that they have a variety of options. Second, the pupil services administrator may convey to all that he or she is a fair person who can see the merits in an opposite point of view when a case is well made and laced with facts. Third, there must be a staff development of team participants so that case materials are reviewed objectively and recommendations made on personal conscience and not because of administrative fiat.

# 10 The Future of Guidance and Counselling

The viability of guidance as a major helping service depends not only on the profusion of societal problems, complexities, and needs; it must be seen as an effective response. The many publics-pupils, parents, legislators, the community at large, and educators-must view guidance as a profession that provides a need service, available from no other source. Two factors determine whether or not this will occur. The first is the sensitivity and perceptiveness of guidance workers in discerning the *real* problems and needs, particularly those of which the general public is only dimly aware. The second is the effectiveness in communicating goals and results to this same public. Obviously something positive has to happen in the lives of those who come in contact with guidance. Identifying needs and publicizing results will not alone accomplish the task of ensuring the support of guidance services. But guidance already has the means to ensure that it has a significant impact, and the dynamic nature of the profession, documented throughout this book, practically guarantees that it will enlarge and improve on present approaches and techniques. Thus, the question needs to be faced, will the guidance professions able to respond effectively to the two major tasks? My position is that it will; the motivation, competency, and imagination of those who will do the job are already plentiful. In fact, a recurring theme in earlier chapters is the inventiveness guidance workers have repeatedly demonstrated not only in dealing with current needs but in anticipating emerging or hidden ones. Failure will come only if enthusiasm falters, and pressures and challenges are allowed to cause a futile search for security through ingratiatingly taking on a myriad of insignificant and irrelevant tasks in the attempt to become indispensable rather than be professional.

Predictions are hazardous but necessary. The task is made easier by the post-Bicentennial climate of taking stock and looking to the future. A positive orientation towards the future is essential in the midst of the present confusions and dilemmas: America is wallowing in a period of disappointment and disillusion. The idea of progress is till alive, but it is not well. There is an emerging 'new pessimism', not only in foreign policy but in domestic affairs. Government is viewed as, inevitably, bumbling and corrupt. Other social institutions are considered obsolete and ineffectual.

But, Elam's view is not one of long-term pessimism. Hopeful signs both of society in general and schools in particular can be drawn from the position that ours is a "self correcting society" and the schools are "a major instrument in shaping the future".

The bases for optimism are substantial. Resources re being depleted, but there are avenues available utilizing selective growth and alternative energy resources that can, if used fully and promptly, head off disaster. The nation's collective ingenuity can find new ways to cope with destructive trends. Scientific and social innovations and breakthroughs have served to improve the quality of life in past years and have the potential for equally or greater success in the future. We are only beginning to use our intellectual potential for progress on all fronts; education, especially, stands to gain enormously from new developments in both the cognitive and affective areas. But we may need to experience a "socioquake" and thus arrive at new ways of viewing man in relation to the environment rather than patching up the old perceptions and practices.

With an assumption of constructive and positive changes, what are major directions for the next several decades? A review of even a handful of the significant themes required a look at political, economic, social, and educational aspects. There is a continuity in the international political alignments among power blocs, even as new nations strive for status and recognition, and energy resources modify relations among countries. International politics will be based on power balances and energy resources, but there will be a greater recognition and acceptance of the concept of interdependence of nations. The related worldwide problems of growth, crowding, and inadequate resources will be faced; cooperative efforts will be made to slow down the population explosion, increase worldwide food production, and enhance the self-sufficiency of third-world countries.

Economic problems, primarily inflation, and unemployment, will continue to cause hardships for individuals, while increasing both the cost of services and the need for them. Cooperation among nations will be emphasized, while reduced energy resources and needs of undeveloped countries heighten problems in this country.

The trend of a rising median population age will continue, and the effects will be felt in every aspect of life. Not only will there be a shift in the emphasis of guidance and counseling, but retirement policies and benefits, education, housing, medical care, and the world of work will be dramatically affected. Work and the work setting are changing in ways that will have profound effects in the years ahead. There will be an increased demand for job security as protection against the fluctuations in the economy. At the same time, however, more humane and stimulating working conditions will be sought. The work week and work day will be shortened, and variations such as splitting job and self-selected work hours will be tested. The increasing age of the labor force and the steady trend for more female participation will affect the workplace in many ways not yet known to us.

Changes in education will range from introducing new financing plans to establishing programs for lifelong learning. As the proportion of school-age individuals decreases, the cost of public education rises, and the needs and political power of older persons become more visible, we may see a higher quality of schooling. It seems certain that there will be provisions for lifelong easy entry and exit in educational and training programs. New school models will merge education and life-family, community, and work-in ways that will make education more significant. Writz predicts that "some kind of prevision for enterprising the earning and learning of a living, for interweaving for interspersing the earning and learning of a living, for interweaving employment and self-renewal, is going to have to be recognized as the essential condition for an effective career as worker, citizen, or human being".

A host of trends are encompassed by the need Shane describes as "how to remotivate youth to feel that life is good, that it is worth living, and that it can bring enduring satisfaction". Many of the problems of today stem from the lacks this statement implies; some young people seek solutions in fads, cults, drugs, or deviant life-styles. The educational institution will play a significant part in building new values and purpose, but the next several decades will be marked more by questions and searching than by answers and solutions.

If we translate the societal trends into guidelines for counseling and guidance, a general picture of increased pressure for services emerges. The need to make the most use possible of human and material resources leads to a greater concern for individual awareness of potential and opportunities. Material resources will be carefully used by those who are sensitive to the needs of others and are aware of the importance of sharing rather than thinking only of themselves.

The increasing interdependence among nations could enhance concern for problems that are common to different cultures and bring guidance workers in different countries closer together to pool strategies and techniques. Developing and underdeveloped countries can profit from learning about what is done in other areas if they have the opportunity to adapt principles and strategies for local uses. It would be well to avoid an attitude that what is done in technologically advanced countries is best for others. A cooperative approach to unique needs of each culture would be true implementation of the spirit of guidance.

Many of the cutbacks that appear to be inevitable will very likely cause disruptions in established patterns of travel ,recreation, and day-to-day living. New modes may actually be growth-producing-there may, for example, be less dependence on commercial entertainment-but the changes may call for difficult adaptations.

The changing age of the population has obvious and important implications for guidance. Not only will there be a shift to include expanded services for those in their middle and later years, but new types of help will be needed, e.g., assisting mid-life and older persons with educational and work planning.

The changing world of work offers some of the most direct implications for guidance and counseling of any aspect of life. Even though efforts are being made to adapt work to individuals and to develop new patterns of work hour and sharing jobs, the central problem of finding meaning and fulfillment will demand increased attention. Perhaps a combination of meaningful leisure activities and income-producing work will needed. Whatever the eventual solutions, it seems that some kind of human development services both the workplace and in the community will be needed.

The changing world of work offers some of the most direct implications for guidance and counseling and aspect of life. Even though efforts are being made to adapt work to individuals and to develop new patterns of work hours and sharing jobs, the central problem of finding meaning and fulfillment will demand increased attention. Perhaps a combination of meaningful leisure activities and income-producing work will be needed. Whatever the eventual solutions, it seems that some kind of human development services both in the workplace and in the community will be needed.

The increasing need for accountability and making the most productive use of resources will make education give additional emphasis to helping all pupils understand and utilize their full potential. Questions are being raised about the assumed benefits of large schools, and there is a shift emerging that emphasizes compulsory education, not just compulsory attendance. These and other trends imply that help will needed to make the school a place for learning and development attuned to the needs of the individual and the community.

The task of helping youth to find challenge, meaning, and stimulation in school programs, work, and productive community life is made even more demanding by the changing social and economic conditions. This is a school-community problem that demands the best efforts of practically everyone, but it is one in which guidance personnel have a unique opportunity for effective leadership and service.

A brief and general review of major trends slights a multitude of specific issues, problems and directions of critical significance for guidance workers (e.g. licensure, ethics, preparation, and affirmative action), but it gives the backdrop against which they will be worked out. Moreover, the major trends contain an formation of an increasing need for guidance and counseling for helping all individuals in lifelong growth and development and to give guidelines for dealing with the specific questions and problems.

**The need for new approaches**

A major point of this book is that new strategies, techniques, and technology are vital of effective delivery of services today. The future will make even greater demands on the creativity and inventiveness of guidance workers. Two factors support this prediction-accountability and financing. From the counselor's point of view, the major reason is to provide better-quality help to more people; improving the quality of life ranks above the demand for hard evidence of effects and adjusting to cope with financial limitations. But the realities of the situation require a consideration of the most effective use of personnel and material resources to achieve desired goals. Tomorrow may usher in strategies that are unknown today.

The past few years have witnessed a proliferating of approaches, technology, and strategies. Some are destined for a brief meteoric life before falling into oblivion. Others are sure to become major styles of guidance in the future. The problem that counselors face is how to tell the difference. There is no quick or easy way; research and evaluation provide the most valid answers. Intuition may seem a trusty guide, but it is often so entangled in personal commitment to an approach or enthusiasm for a cause that its value is doubtful.

Moreover, the attitude that what is new is new is good and what is old is bad leads to a distorted view that inhibits a thoughtful and perceptive selection of the most effective means. This naive position, coupled with a tendency to partially try out and quickly dispose of new approaches, not only creates discontinuous development but often relegates to the scrap heap potentially valuable methods and materials. There is much faddishness in U. S. guidance, abetted by an affluence that permits spending of enormous sums on new developments that are discarded even before rigorous testing can be completed. This luxury is fast disappearing. It will take careful evaluation and use of both the old and new to fashion the guidance of the future.

Productive elements that will gain additional use in the years ahead are reflected in earlier chapters. Consultation is one. Together with psychological education and "giving guidance away", it represents a new taking shape for many years. Paraprofessional and computers also have great potential. The needs survey, a new label for holding guidance close to what the public wants, is obviously here to stay. It has never disappeared since the concept of guidance first surfaced at the turn of the century, but since then it has fallen on hard times. Accountability is of course not new; the only surprising things is that it took so long to emerge as a major consideration in the helping services. A number of other strategies have been endorsed in the preceding pages; the movement toward lifelong learning and guidance, and integrating the school with the community and workplace are the most significant. The separate elements are not new, but the synthesis brings into being a strategy of tremendous importance.

One front along which the profession advances does not involve largescale movements nationwide in scope-it is in the day-to-day work of the counselor who may, for example, develop a better way to help a counselee explore goals, make decisions, and carry out plans, or devise a new mode of working with groups of pupils or parents. It could be any of the mutitude of things the counselor does. Shared with colleagues, these activities have a ripple effect that eventually makes a difference in school guidance.

Some trends appear to be fairly clearly indicated by current developments. One of these is licensure. There almost certainly will be some type of widespread provisions for licensure, which will have an impact on school counselors. Effects will be felt more definitely by those in non-school gettings, however, as it is predicted that employment in an educational institution will enable the counselor to practice regardless of licensure status.

Accountability will be given more attention in all settings. Evidence of positive effects will be needed to ensure the continued existence of school guidance services as well as to maintain support for programs in other settings. Moreover, counselors will be expected to expand services with little additional financial support.

The counselor's role will be more clearly defined, partly because of accountability and partly because of the use of new strategies such as outreach and psychological education, which give the work a visible structure and purpose.

Increasing attention will be given to the needs of special groups, e.t., mid-life and older persons, minorities, the handicapped, and women. Moreover, we will see at least the beginning of the implementation of lifelong learning and school-community cooperative approaches. Changes in public education, particularly the expanded infusion of career education, will make the school a more dynamic and realistic learning environment. At the same time the "basics" will be increasingly emphasized. All of these changes will offer counselors opportunities to serve in new ways and to build a solid position in education.

More processes and personnel will be utilized to expand the reach of guidance services. Paraprofessionals are one example, particularly peer counselors. After their slow start in the past decade, computers will be used with increasing frequency.

As school budgets are examined, questions will be raised about the necessity for guidance services. The predicted outcome, however, is that there will be an increase in the support for services because the offer ways to deal with the most pressing school and community problems.

The impact of the social, economic, and political trends described on pp. 342-345 will have a more pronounced effect on guidance and counseling than in the immediate future. It is predicted that more definite patterns of those trends given for the next five years will have emerged, e.g., licensure regulations will be crystallized, career education will be the major mode in public education, and guidance roles will be more clear-cut and more widely understood. Computer technology will be used, and counselors will have much more time to devote to the personal, effective, and decision-making needs of youth.

Lifelong education and school-community cooperation will be realities, and counselors will work with all ages in both school and community. There will be increases in the number of counselors needed; preparation standards will provide for differential staffing, with high levels of technical and human-relations competency for those in supervisory positions. At the same time there will be increased attention to prevention of problems and the provision of easily available community-wide services. School counselors will be regarded as logical persons to coordinate all school-guidance and pupil-personnel services, and will provide leadership for community-wide coordination strategies.

*Guidance beyond the year 2000*

Disregarding the gloomy projections of those who question the likelihood of civilization lasting into the 21st century-such apprehension would have been equally appropriate in any approach of recorded history-it is not only possible but essential to look ahead to try to discern a reasonably accurate, if tentative, outline of the shape of guidance. Leaders in the field, such as Berdie, Harris, Morgan, and Walz, show a substantial consensus about major developments in the future. Four characteristics stand out. First, the counselor will go where people are; outreach will be major strategy, and there will be considerable use of support persons. Marple describes a thought provoking fantasy of the future in which "Friendship Centers" alter the lives of people nationally and internationally. But typically, no clear-cut definition of the arrangement of such a center is given; but the implication is that location and type of housing will be of less importance than what happens in the community.

The second major prediction is that services will be available lifelong; the school-age emphasis will have disappeared. Guidance will be provided over the whole range of individuals and groups; no social strata or subculture will be favored over any other. Along with this breadth, helping agencies and institutions will collaborate far more than they do today, and guidance workers will have a more comprehensive knowledge of and better working relationships with, colleagues in other settings.

Much of the counselor's work will emphasize

prevention; while crisis help will be provided, the major thrust will be the change agent's task reducing or eliminating destructive features of the environment that generate problems.

The counselor's increased versatility will require a sound background in theory, research, and techniques, the quality of preparation will rise. Facilitating personal development, building effective working relationships, and gaining an in-depth understanding of various cultures will be given higher priority. Preparation programs will utilize input from the school, the community, and the working world, and measure student progress on the basis of competency. Other aspects of the role in the years ahead involve legal status, ethical practices, professional organizations, and counselor's supply and demand. Prospects are good for increased professional status and the attendant legal and ethical responsibilities. Professional organizations will again the prestige to induce employers to upgrade hiring standards. Some form of licensure will be in operation; counselors will participate in setting qualifications and examining applicants. It is very probable that counselors will be completely in charge of this process.

Expansions in the directions predicted here-lifelong service, and broad applications in life areas-will mean that the demand for counselors will exceed the supply. Notwithstanding changes in support at the federal and state levels, and increased competition for available funds, the need for counselors will be so apparent and the efforts of guidance so well documented, that ample financing will be forthcoming and opportunities for employment will be plentiful.

# Index